# THE
# EMERGING
# CITY

# THE EMERGING CITY

## Myth and Reality

with a new introduction by
Janet Abu-Lughod

## Scott Greer

Transaction Publishers
New Brunswick (U.S.A.) and London (U.K.)

New material this edition copyright © 1999 by Transaction Publishers, New Brunswick, New Jersey 08903. Originally published in 1962 by The Free Press.

This book is printed on acid-free paper that meets the American National Standard for Permanence of Paper for Printed Library Materials.

Library of Congress Catalog Number: 98-11414
ISBN: 0-7658-0432-8
Printed in the United States of America

Library of Congress Cataloging-in-Publication Data

Greer, Scott A.
    The emerging city : myth and reality / Scott Greer ; with a new introduction by Janel Abu-Lughod.
        p.  cm.
    Originally published: New York : Free Press, 1962. With new introd.
    Includes bibliographical references and index.
    ISBN 0-7658-0432-8 (pbk. : alk. paper)
    1. Sociology, Urban.  I. Title.
HT151.G68   1998
307.76—dc21
                                                                98-11414
                                                                CIP

# CONTENTS

# INTRODUCTION TO THE TRANSACTION EDITION

**I**T was a remarkable experience to reread my worn copy of the original edition of this prescient book, which occupies a permanent place in my library—not only because the book is (almost) clairvoyant, but also because I felt in easy dialogue with its author. It seemed as if we were picking up conversations we had carried on intermittently when we were colleagues at Northwestern University in the late 1960s and early 1970s. His mind was rapier sharp, his wit legendary, and his vision—well, wide enough, as might be expected from the poet he always was. I recall that he attributed his vision—I think he called it peripheral vision—to the wide open spaces of Texas where he grew up, and I have, in my mind's memory, traced some of his pessimism about urban change to the time he returned from a visit to Sweetwater and wistfully reported that a gas station now stood in place of the house in which he had grown up. Concern with change was always at the very core of his scholarship.

Careful researcher and lucid writer, Scott Greer never lost sight of the largest questions of human existence: what needs for fellowship and freedom were bedrock? What would be gained and what would be lost as society changed? What kinds of urban settlements were "good" for humans? That is what makes his books worth rereading, in the way that the best writings of philosophers live on, even though the world has gone through countless iterations since the time they wrote. In Scott Greer's case, that world has changed, for the most part, in directions he predicted, even if he "missed" some themes whose importance has since come to the fore. But if he had caught *all* of them, he would have left no work for the rest of us to do. And much work certainly remains, since the changes that have taken place in the world during the generation since this book was written have moved at an ever more rapid pace.

In the 1962 book reprinted here, under the heading of "The Crisis," he bemoaned that, "Some forty years after urban sociologists began their intensive study of the city and political scientists became empirical students of public administration and political behavior, our image of the city is in a process of dissolution" (p. 20). Now, some 35 years *after* he wrote this, the image (and the object) is still dissolving, or at least transmuting in ways his book tries to capture. And to continue this quotation, he complained that, "There is little order in our theories, and our data seem largely irrelevant to them" (ibid.). That indictment, too, still has validity. Perhaps our failures come from the sheer vastness of a topic that in the years since his book was written has encompassed more and more of the essence of life in this ever-connecting world.

*The Emerging City* attempted to advance a theory of society within which the changing city could be interpreted at its social, economic, political, and symbolic levels. The most powerful of his theoretical concepts remains the idea of "increasing scale," which he adapted from a 1945 book by a pair of Africanists, Godfrey and Monica Wilson. Through his personal contacts with Eshref Shevky and Wendell Bell, Scott infused the early work of social area analysts with this overarching metatheory of directional social change and, in *The Emerging City*, he applies the concept to the expanding scale of the metropolis: no longer politically governable by the conventional institutions which have been fragmented by physical boundaries and broken into "communities of limited liability"; no longer relatively autonomous economically but embedded in national and even international developments; no longer places with common "ways of life," as Wirth had predicted, but highly diversified social groupings not adequately comprehended under the terms of rural, urban, and suburban.

Most of these themes are now in such common usage that we almost forget the contributions that Scott Greer made to our understandings. Some of his insights may now seem obvious, but they were certainly not when he first described them. He predicted what I have termed (in my *Changing Cities,* 1991) "saturation urbanization," the phenomenon of a fully urbanized society. Today, four-fifths of Americans live in urbanized areas and the rest are subject to the cultural dominance of its media and tastes. He predicted, as the most recent 1990 census confirmed, that a majority of Americans would be suburbanites (although he failed to recognize how diversified suburbs would become). He even predicted "edge cities," long before that term came into parlance.

It would be unfair to have expected him to predict everything, however, and I have been asked by the editor of this series to point to those areas that need updating. If I do this in the following paragraphs, it is not with the intent to minimize Scott Greer's insights, but to emphasize how many more consequences of "increasing scale" we are now experiencing than his crystal ball, clear as it was, could not yet reveal fully.

Implicit in the book is a recognition that an increase in scale would inevitably integrate more of the world within a common system; in that sense, it hints at the newer work being done on global cities. Shall we quibble with him that his work is unduly centered on America and that, therefore, there is a neglect of the ways global cities would be infused by international "restructuring"? The early 1960s were still at the beginning of such a process, and the United States remained unquestioningly hegemonic, at least until the mid-1960s, before Europe and especially Asia began to compete, economically and culturally.

The concern he showed for a possible leveling down into mass culture was legitimate (Coca Cola everywhere), but his confidence in the "Americanization" of cities and suburbs was misplaced. However, how could he have predicted that the Hart-Celler Act of 1965 would open the doors to massive immigration from non-European culture areas, thus reinfusing the largest American cities with an ethnic diversity he thought was, for better or worse, disappearing?

His predictions for increased "familism" in America also seem quite dated at this point, as the postwar generation that produced the baby boom passes from the scene, leaving in its wake drastically declining fertility, much greater labor force participation by women, and even feminism and its backlash. But we must remember that Betty Friedan's *Feminine Mystique*, often credited with arousing sleepy suburban housewives, was not even published until the late 1960s.

A final blind spot in the book, suggesting that even the clearest eye has an occasional mote, is harder to excuse, especially from an author who in 1959 published *Last Man In: Racial Access to Union Power.* The Civil Rights movement, albeit not yet "popularized," was already deeply engaged by the early 1950s, even though it was then being played out in the courts, rather than in the streets. This movement, barely acknowledged in *The Emerging City*, would have repercussions in the cities and suburbs of America that could be explained neither by a theory of increasing scale nor by the simple "dimension" that social area analysts had called "ethnicity." I find the neglect of racial discrimination and exclusion the only deep flaw in this otherwise wonderful book.

In his defense, he was not alone in underestimating the explosive potential of racism. Few works in urban sociology/politics at that time recognized that the American disease of racism would not be easily cured, and that the "two societies" later described by the 1968 Kerner Report would defy solution and continue to shape our emerging cities. I suspect that if Scott Greer were alive today and revising this work, he would be rewriting and expanding, with his usual insight, this part of theory and change which was largely overlooked in his time.

Very little else in this stunning work would require revision. That, in itself, is ample reason for Transaction Publishers to reprint it and for all young urbanists to read this "classic" work in urban studies.

Janet Abu-Lughod
New York, 1998

# ACKNOWLEDGMENTS

PARTS of several chapters have appeared elsewhere in an earlier form. "Order and Change in Metropolitan Society" derives from a paper with the same title given at the Conference on Educational Policy in a Metropolitan Society, sponsored by the Council on Educational Administration and The Center for Metropolitan Studies, Northwestern University, 1959; it appears in the volume, *Education in Urban Society*, edited by Bob Chandler and John Kitsuse (to be published, 1962). Some parts of "The Citizen in the Urban World" appeared earlier in the essay, "Individual Participation in Mass Society," first published in *Approaches to the Study of Poli-*

*tics,* Roland Young, Editor, Northwestern University Press, 1959. "The Community of Limited Liability" derives to a considerable degree from the article, "The Social Structure and Political Process of Suburbia," first published in the *American Sociological Review*, 24:514-526. Some of the material in Chapters VI and VII first appeared in a paper, "Social Change and the Metropolitan Problem," presented at the Third Annual Faculty Seminar on Metropolitan Research Problems, sponsored jointly by the Maxwell Graduate School of Syracuse University and the National Committee on Government Finance of the Brookings Institution (August, 1961). It appears in the *Report* of that Seminar. I am grateful to the Public Affairs Program of the Ford Foundation for supporting much of the research upon which this volume is based, as well as support during the academic year 1961-62, when the final version was completed.

The individual scholars whose work has helped me in reaching the conclusions presented here are too numerous to name. Some of them are (inadequately) acknowledged in the notes to these chapters. I am perhaps most indebted to four older men, young Turks all (though only the first can claim a strict right to that title): Eshref Shevky, Norton Long, David Riesman, and Fred Cottrell. Needless to add, they are not responsible for what I've done with their ideas.

# THE CITY
# IN CRISIS

CHAPTER 1

OURS IS AN URBAN WORLD. In a way that has never been true in the past we have given all of our hostages to the encompassing fortunes of great cities. Imperial Rome under the Augustans may have been as much as 10 per cent urban; America today is over 60 per cent urban and nearly half of the urbanites live in metropolitan areas with populations of over one million. Projecting these present tendencies into the future, an estimate made in 1960 indicates that four-fifths of the great increase in population expected by 1980

1

will be metropolitan, with the urban proportion of the total over 70 per cent.[1] Thus, there is little chance for most of us to escape from the city, even should we wish to; we had better begin to try to understand it.

This is a difficult assignment. It is very much as though we were studying the geography of the earth in the planet's early days, when cataclysmic change took place continually in response to pressure and heat, under cover of a nearly continuous cloud of vapor produced by the very changes we wished to observe. The nature of the city is changing, and the very rapidity of change is producing conflict and confusion in our images and our policy. Yet we must work out trial solutions; intellectual and political decisions are demanded every day and will not wait upon a final solution. Ironically and inescapably, our policy is one of the dynamics altering the city, and our policy rests upon our images of the city, our notions of how it works and of possible instruments for change and control.

## Some Policy Choices

Our choices begin with the emerging shape of the metropolis itself. Though much is inherited, the funded energy of the past in the shape of the vast physical plant of the city does not foreclose all future choice: the projected growth for the next two decades insures that. One possibility is the retention of the general focus and structure of the city as we have inherited it. This is a more difficult job than may appear on the surface, for the original settlers, speculators, entrepreneurs, and peculators built in terms of a technology and a society that are no more. Much of the inherited city is made up of overvalued and obsolete slums, loft buildings, and nineteenth-century factories, their access barricaded by traffic. What are the possibilities of retaining such a structure for the city, what are the costs, and what are the benefits?

How should we channel new growth, and how can we do so? While urban redevelopment has resulted in a few monuments and failures dedicated to the salvage of the older parts of the city, the increasing population of the metropolis has busily built and inhabited its own version of "greenbelts" in the suburbs. Most of the metropolitan growth since World War II has been suburban development, and of the population growth of sixty-four million expected by 1980, over 80 per cent will be in the suburbs. Thus, the channeling of new growth competes for attention with conservation and rebuilding of older areas.[2]

A key question for consideration by either viewpoint, and one that is frequently a bone of contention between partisans of the Utopias, is traffic and transportation. What will the circulatory system of the metropolis be? Will the increasing automobile traffic force an increase in the arteries, further adjustment to the automobile as chief carrier, and thus increasing numbers of automobiles? Such a course leads public transportation into the vicious circle of fewer passengers, greater per capita cost, poor service, higher fares, fewer passengers—and a continuous encouragement to use the automobile. On the other hand, what combination of statute and the public fisc can rechannel transportation? The last war was effective, since it literally prohibited automobile traffic through rationing.

Nothing else has been effective. Those committed to public transportation point out, however, that little else has been tried—while the cities subsidize the automobile drivers and the latter flourish under such subsidy.

The automobile has, as one virtue, its great ability to increase the accessibility of scattered places on the periphery of the city: suburbia is auto-borne. Suburbia is also, preponderantly, native-born and white. Those who live in the older portions of the city (and who are, in a sense, conservatives of an older urban tradition) are of a different complexion. As their numbers increase, in absolute terms, and as they become a higher proportion of the residents and voters, they increasingly make their needs felt. The growing number of ethnic residents in the limited area of the central city has often been interpreted through the classic law of gases—and many observers await, with trepidation, the day when the central city "blows its top." Struggles to break and to hold the legal and extralegal barriers used in the war of containment are continuous—they are not unrelated to the suburban movement of the white population. These struggles create continuous policy problems in the central city—and it is no wonder that mayors and race relations commissions look with some bitterness upon the suburbanites, who profit from the total work and wealth of the metropolis but refuse to share its costs.

Yet the central city also continues to produce the classic problems of urban democracy along with the wealth from which suburbia derives its income. Few of the great public parks that grace our cities are safe at night—and many are dangerous at high noon. Entire neighborhoods are the scenes of guerilla war, with *freikorps* battling for the control of the streets. The safety of person and property is not automatically assured in the greatest cities of the wealthiest nation. The battle to naturalize the immigrant and acculturate the unwashed continues, and with it the battle to civilize, through civil service and administrative law, the political and governmental organizations of the city.

These are difficult problems, for they demand solutions considering both arguments of equity and knowledge of means. Perhaps the most encompassing statement of the urban policy choice is simply: what governmental form is best suited to contain and resolve the issues that have been lightly touched on above, as well as those not mentioned and the myriads that are surely moving toward us over the horizon of history? What is the relevant constituency? What structure can both represent the interests that demand representation and, at the same time, resolve the ineluctable conflicts inherent in the contemporary metropolis?

These are only a few of the policy choices faced by the metropolis today.

## The Kaleidoscope of Images

Decisions on such topics are intimately related to the guiding image, the over-all theory, with which we approach the city. How shall we effectively focus this particular "booming, buzzing confusion," this complex mass of heterogeneous and transient human action moving through time? How shall we summarize patterns in a limited set of categories, so that we can relate the parts in a meaningful way?

The development of a coherent body of thought with respect to such a large and immediate subject usually begins with a metaphor. Whether it develops into a scientifically established theory or remains a metaphor, such an image provides at least a rudimentary concept, a handle for intellectual control. With respect to the metropolis, then, we may ask: What kinds of metaphors dominate our intellectual discourse? What images stand for the totality and are, for practical purposes, "theories of the city"? We shall begin by inspecting the images used by social scientists who are concerned with the city. Political scientists, economists, and sociologists have for many decades manifested a continuing interest in the urban complex.

Political scientists typically approach the city as a governmental unit with powers and duties of a specific kind. From the concern of classical theorists with the city state, from consideration of the importance of the city in the development of modern law, and from day-to-day concern with the administrative structure of urban government, they inherit a rich body of information and concepts. The city, for the political scientist, is the corporate body, the legal personality, a little prototype of the state, preceding in history the development of the nation. It rests upon a balance of power among contending interests (including the interest of the prince) and its product is the polity: order, roads, monuments, and the "authoritative allocation of values" by those with legitimate power.

Urban sociologists emphasize a geographical image of

the city. Under the influence of the ecological approach, they have constructed a two dimensional theory of the city—a sprawling map of people in places Theirs has been a metaphor emphasizing the unplanned, "blind" development of urban concentration, the regularities in the use of space that are unlegislated but enforced by mechanisms of competition for *lebensraum*. The city, for the urban ecologist, is the mass of population, heterogeneous and dense, segregated by wealth and cultural background. It is a loose congeries with a vestigial normative structure, existing like "nature's half acre" in an ecological balance. One of the competing groups is government itself—parties, patrons, officials. Although the early ecologists paid tribute to a moral order coexistent with the ecological order, the research and theory of urban sociology shows little concern for such a dimension. The equilibrium of their city rests upon an ecological balance among contending subgroups, and its product is a division of labor and rewards reflected on a map.

The economists, late comers to the study of the city, see it in two lights. First, as a matrix of locations for firms —a necessary translation of a national economy into space. Second, and more pertinent to our inquiry, some economists have been turning toward an image of the city as an economic unit—a kind of super firm, based upon relations between importers and exporters, contractors and subcontractors (with the household as the smallest firm) all involved in an import-export business. Thus, the economist sees the city as a center of production, trade, and distribution, whose basic units are economic organizations. Local government is itself a peculiar kind of firm. The economic city rests upon a division of labor among firms, competition, and cooperation within the framework of the market, with advantages and disadvantages in the form of location, multipliers, and marginal economies. The city as a whole is "in business," and its economic position may be estimated by the balance of trade.

All three of these images of the city betray the heavy hand of nineteenth-century liberalism. Although the political theorists concerned with the city sometimes misplaced their concreteness, mistaking a territorial jurisdiction for a general and universal social structure, when it came to business matters their city was rigorously limited to the constitutionally established powers and forms of city government in the United States. In the same fashion, the assumptions of laissez faire are built into the ecological image. Competition, conflict, accommmodation and assimilation take place within a framework of rules approximately the same as those advocated by Herbert Spencer—with room for social evolution, enterprise, and the survival of those most fit to survive. The economic image is simply a verbatim translation: the city becomes a small business man.

Today, all three of these approaches suffer from the same limitation: they are far too partial. Each makes assumptions basic to its explanatory power that are never defined and tested; all focus upon the city without much concern for its environment in social space and time. In order to improve explanation and prediction in particular cases, each is extended toward the bounds of the others (frequently moving past the center of the neighboring discipline, with comic results). In the process of extension the clarity of the original image, a major virtue, is lost in the confusion of "interdisciplinary" thought. The image becomes encrusted with a mass of *ad hoc* barnacles, epicycles, and hemidemisemiquavers.

Thus, the political scientist finds that his approach leads from classic political theory to the constitutional form of municipal government with at least moderate success, but the day to day operations of government force him to look at the nongovernmental norms that determine behavior—including the folkways and mores of avoiding the law. He is led still further afield by his concern with political parties: how can one explain governmental behavior without explaining party organization? Party organization, without economic interests? And this subject is closely related to the ecologist's concern with kinds of people in space, the conflict of group interests (including the interests of firms), the accommodations that are improvised and form the basis for tradition and, perhaps, law.

When the political scientist turns to look at the city today, he finds that the corporate body is broken into dozens of separate entities: the central city is enmeshed in a web of suburbs, a tangle of villages. Yet this is still, in some sense, "one city." Now he must consider the consequences of ecological shifts in a new light: the suburbs become overwhelmingly white, higher in social class, tending toward Republican affiliation. The central city becomes an electorate of working-class and ethnic identity. Yet each is a necessary condition for the other's existence. Furthermore, the public fisc itself is affected. The "city" may be viewed as a firm, one that can prosper or go bankrupt. Public administration theory can be related to Taylorism and the theory of the firm. Yet this firm's customers are voters, and it may be forced to do business at a constant loss.

The urban ecologist has similar problems. The urban map changes, and frequently the change forces one to look at governmental action—the moral order. Urban redevelopment, zoning, governmental autonomy in the suburbs, such matters as these change the land values of the city but cannot be explained by simple competition for space. At the same time the city, as entrepreneur, struggles to control its own economic future through promotion, redevelopment, the construction of "industrial parks." The roots of these developments lie in areas of economic and political organization that are hardly amenable to exploration through census data plotted on maps, yet they affect the maps. They represent, in some sense, an urban polity—something missing from nature's half acre.

The economist's emerging image suffers similar sea changes. He is forced to grant that zoning laws may shut off the choicest locations for industrial plants, may at an extreme impoverish a metropolitan area, while the general level of governmental services and taxes may affect the recruitment of industry to an area and hence the economic development of the city. The public fisc becomes a necessary but theoretically indigestible part of his apparatus. At the same time, if he is interested in welfare, he is forced to note that governmental services make up an area of consumption in which American urban populations frequently have static or declining products to consume. The competitive market does not produce streets, police protection, playgrounds, and parks. Here the *polity* is analagous to the market. The economist must become a student of political science in order to answer strictly economic questions.

Equally as damaging, however, as the partiality of these approaches, is the limitation in scope. A generally useful image should allow one to summarize the pertinent detail and explain cases varying widely in their surface nature; it should thus allow the interpretation of change through time. While it would be in process of continual modification and improvement, moving toward the condition of a theory, it could not be casually jettisoned. Yet Martindale, in a recent essay on Max Weber's approach to the city, indicates grave doubts as to the usefulness of the image developed by this major and influential sociologist (who was also, and originally, a political economist).

Max Weber's theory of the city, thus, leads to a rather interesting conclusion. We can grant the phenomenal increase and aggregation of modern populations as a concomitant of the industrial revolution. We should not, however, confuse physical aggregation with the growth of the city in a sociological sense. The urban community has everywhere lost its military integrity—its right to defend itself by military means. In many areas of the world it has, temporarily at least, lost its very legal and political autonomy—the same fate is possible everywhere. Meanwhile, within the city itself greater masses of residents pursue interlocal interests—as representatives of the national government, as agents in business and industries of national and international rather than of civic scope.

The modern city is losing its external and formal structure. Internally it is in a state of decay while the new community represented by the nation everywhere grows at its expense. The age of the city seems to be at an end.[3]

This statement indicates one writer's belief that the utility of the legal-social definition of the city is at an end —that the city has no separate existence and therefore no interest for the social scientist. That this is not a parochial conclusion is indicated by Albert Reiss, in an introduction to one of the most authoritative collections of readings in urban sociology.

> There seems to be a decline of interest in research on cities and city life, if the research in urban demography and human ecology is excluded from consideration. This is in part due to the fact that much of the research simply considers the urban community to be a *context* within which a particular kind of theoretical problem is studied, but the context itself is not often made the object of investigation. . . . A second reason for the decline in urban research activity is the fact that there has been a shift in the problem-area division of sociological knowledge so that certain of the problems formerly conceptualized as "urban sociology" now are viewed within another frame of reference or theory. This is true, for example, of what now are called the problem fields of industrial sociology, social stratification and mass communication. There is some reason to believe that the sociology of city life will limit itself largely to a consideration of urban structure (in the sense of community) during the next decade and that the fragmentation of the field will continue.[4]

Thus, Martindale counsels the abandonment of the city as a usable image of whatever kind, while for Reiss the city as an independent object of study becomes a study of community, from which concern with work, social class, mass communications, and other aspects of life in cities are eliminated. Surely this would also eliminate most of the sociological relevance of the metropolis. Ironically, at the point in time when the city has reached a societal dominance never before seen, it seems to elicit confessions of theoretical bankruptcy from its students.

For the economist, too, the city may cease to be a basic unit of analysis. Raymond Bernon concludes from a recent study of the New York Metropolitan Region that

> we are a nation tending toward regional self-sufficiency in the production of goods. The plants in each region are developing increasingly complex ties with one another. And although they are not showing any increasing tendency to settle within the borders of metropolitan areas, nevertheless one of the major determinants of their location is the size and location of these metropolitan clusters.[5]

The overweening centralization of many economic activities in cities is, in this view, declining; in its place a considerably larger geographical area (without any of the classic characteristics of cities save economic interdependence), becomes the most useful unit for studying the problems of local economies.

## The City and Mass Society

Thus, the images of the city deteriorate as the structure of the larger society alters through time: the economic city expands and diffuses, the political city loses autonomy and is merged in the national polity, the social city becomes indistinct from the larger whole, a context, a sample of modern society. This leads to another view of the city—that which identifies the city and nation, summarizing both under the rubric of "mass society." Such an image does not allow one to differentiate the city from all that is most characteristic of contemporary society nor, on the other hand, does it encourage one to investigate the internal structure of the city. It moves from vast changes in the nation to transformations of the individual.

Ortega, Spengler, Durkheim, Tonnies, these are some of the ideologues who saw the city as the summation of contemporary society, the end product of a long process transforming the ethnic groups of band and village into megalopolitan society.[6] Ortega saw the hierarchical orders crumbling beneath the waves of economic and political democracy, and prophesied the state of the masses; western culture would perish under the onslaught of the vulgar. Spengler spoke of the death of culture in the cities of the Autumn, social products of a loss of nerve that would lead, in the end, to Caesarism and the deification of massive power. Durkheim saw the city as epitomizing the social dust heap, the organic society unified by interdependence through the division of labor, but producing an unstable unity in which consensus and solidarity are partial and problematic. Tonnies saw community give way to the urban world in which most bonds are instrumental, negotiable, contractual, while rights and duties become separated from the age-old sanctification of the community and its rewards.

Such is the image of the city as product and producer of mass society: like the magic salt mill that sank, still grinding, to the bottom of the ocean, the city processes the culture and way of life of modern man until the entire sea has been salted. It is an image particularly congruent with American folk thought; the small-town bias of American sociologists and the important rural survivals in urban American culture led many scholars to give credence to the mass image of the urban world, even before the limitations of the various partial analyses noted had become apparent. After all, Lincoln Steffens (still a revered commentator on urban life) became famous for his study, *The Shame of the Cities* and Lord Bryce spoke of American urban government as our most conspicuous failure. Carl Sandburg immortalized an earlier Chicago as "wicked," "crooked," "brutal," while Theodore Dreiser (in his novels based upon the career of Yerkes) made dramatic and credible a view of the city as a veritable jungle in which power was evil, virtue weak, and the community notable for its absence. Such an image of the city combined the view of the countryman, the frustrated reformer, and the laissez-faire liberal of Spencerian proclivities with the powerful poetry of the ideologues.[7] Ralph Borzodi raised the flat question, *Are Cities Abnormal?* and Lewis Mumford looked back in nostalgia to the communes of the thirteenth century. This pessimistic view attained academic respectability during the 1930's, particularly in the field called "Social Disorganization."[8]

The movement in American sociology to group the scattered studies of "social problems" in the more general field of social disorganization coincided roughly with the great depression. This approach referred all "problems" back to a general illness or incompetence of the social structure; pathological in its focus, it implicitly defined as the normal, healthy society the small town of an earlier America—or even the peasant community and the folk society. This use of a "rural-urban continuum" within which to organize and "explain" a heterogeneous mass of social problems resulted in a ubiquitous bias against the city—while the nation was rapidly becoming urbanized. Although such an approach usually paid lip service to processes of reorganization, the image of the city as the summation of social disorganization left precious little room for stability, order, and reconstruction.

The acceptance of such an image by urban sociologists was not unrelated to the ecological image of the city: it was nourished upon statistics indicating the concentration of crime, suicide, divorce, and other "social pathologies" in the cities as well as the various small studies of Chicago carried out under the direction and inspiration of Robert Park. Pictures of the urban extremes, the "Gold Coast," the slums, the "black belt," the "hobohemia," emphasized the dramatic variety of situations to be found in a metropolitan area.[9] Most important of all, however, was the celebrated essay of Louis Wirth, "Urbanism as a Way of Life," in which Wirth defines the city as a large, dense, permanent settlement of unlike groups and derives from these attributes certain likely patterns of interaction and their consequences: impersonality, isolation, the decline of primary group membership, and the dominance of formal organizations.[10] These are seen as the social characteristics of the city and, by extension, of the contemporary mass society.

Upon such a basis was the "massified" image of the city formulated and built into many urban-sociology textbooks.

Such a view was probably related to the general *weltschmerz* of the deep depression: poverty, unemployment, deficit financing at home; dictatorship, purges, and, above all, the imminence of war abroad. The doctrine of the mass society and the image of the massified city corresponded to a belief in societal determinism reciprocal to the loss of *naive* faith in individual effort. The failure of men to control history in the light of their values was evident on every hand, while Marxism and other forms of historical evolutionism focused attention upon the patterns of the failure. The dissolution of consensus and the collapse of the Republic in Germany; the dramatic quality of mass persuasion used by the demagogues of the right and the left; the power of class and race as tools for organizing social power—these were some of the regular occurrences that bulked so large in the consciousness of the 1930's. Nowhere is this stated more succinctly than in Lederer's book on Hitler, *State of the Masses*, at once a technical analysis and an appreciation of that demagogue's use of the destructive forces inherent in modern, urban society.[11] Awareness of them permeated the social thought of the thirties.

The image of the massified city during the depression was one that was closely related to an image of the total society; yet the American society of the 1930's was also one in which a variety of welfare efforts were under way; the New Deal not only publicized need, it symbolized an evolving polity that tendered means toward amelioration. Pare Lorentz and Lewis Mumford made their spectacular film, "The City," emphasizing the negative judgments of contemporary urban life—but the public-works projects poured millions of man-hours into reconstruction of the city. The mass image never served an eschatological function for American thinkers; their roots in a pragmatic and ameliorative culture were too strong for this. And, once the depression and the war had passed, the image and the reality for which it stood moved very nearly 180 degrees, from moral rejection to acceptance.

In the ten years after World War II a number of influential books appeared, dealing, again, with mass society and the city—but with what a difference! In the works of David Riesman and his associates, as well as those of William Holley White, Samuel Lubell, A. C. Spectorsky, and John R. Seeley, the image of the existing mass society very closely approaches earlier utopias.[12] While the poor remain with us, they are much fewer, and a general ebullience of tone implies their eventual disappearance. While American urban life is mobile and therefore rootless in an older sense, it appears likely that shallow roots will do the trick, even roots like those of certain water plants, which allow the plants wide latitude to drift on a liquid surface. And the political apathy, the vulnerability to charisma and manipulation, the *rassenkampf,* the resentment against the social order? They are either cured by twenty years of economic expansion, or else made orderly and predictable by the twin engines of the mass market and the mass media. (As Wallace Stevens once wrote: ". . . Oxidia, banal suburb / One-half of all its installments paid . . . Oxidia is Olympia.")

In all of these works the mass society is practically identified with the massified city; however, there is a striking change in focus. No longer is the older central city the arena in which good and evil grapple in a dozen matches; instead, the center of the mass is now suburbia. The mass society, the crowds of the street, are located far from the warrens of revolution and crime. They are installed, more or less securely, in the ranks of the middle classes.

This image may be called that of the "mass society in an economy of plenty," as contrasted to the "mass society of deprivation." Its principle characteristics are a continuous and easy upward mobility or, as an alternative, a secure and easy access to the goods of the mass market, for all of the population—this in combination with a wide area of choice in articles of consumption, residence, "culture," social interaction itself. The rules for obtaining the abundance of this cornucopia, however, are rather limiting at the individual level as they are not clearly understood at the societal level. In general, the resident of the massified city is portrayed as committed to (and conforming to) the bureaucratic norms in his place of work, the uncodified norms of his peer group, the continuous bombardment of norms from the mass media. He is, in short, a conformist. Riesman attempts to relate these patterns to changes in the organization of the total society, and to trace the consequences in the institutional areas of work, play, politics, and the like. Whyte emphasizes the social structure of the modern corporation and its consequences for the social character and life style of its employees. The authors of *Crestwood Heights* focus upon the interlocked mechanisms of neighborhood and school as sources of conformity. It is an image of the city that has structural components very similar to those of the "mass society" predicted by the gloomy prophets of the depression, but the over-all color and tone are very different. The degree to which this is caused by a real difference in the nature of the city and the degree to which it is colored by the eyes of the observer remain to be seen.

## The Crisis

Some forty years after urban sociologists began their intensive study of the city and political scientists became empirical students of public administration and political behavior, our image of the city is in a process of dissolution. While we are far richer in heterogeneous concepts and partial theories, as well as information of one kind and another, in crucial ways we are curiously poverty stricken. There is little order in our theories, and our data seem largely irrelevant to them. At the very point in time when we become a metropolitan society, when the problems of the metropolis excite widespread interest, study, and action, some of the scholars studying the city lean toward the notion that it has disappeared while others proffer images so disparate and discrepant that they hardly seem to refer to the same elephant.

The city is a struggle of interest groups, an administrative hierarchy working toward the perfect machine in a curious isolation from politics, or a population whose behavior may be studied as manifestations of power at least as readily as any other aggregate. Or, it is a vast piling up of people with various characteristics, literally, a social "dust heap," organized only in the myriad competing and accommodating subgroups whose arbiter is the market. Or, it is a complex of firms, whose orientation is toward supply, production, marketing, and the advantages of location. Alternatively, it is a spatially defined segment of the total society, a sample of the mass, moving toward anarchy, anomie, revolution and dictatorship—or toward conformism, simple-minded cultural uniformity, prosperity, and bureaucratic rule. Some of these images are in direct conflict, assuming polar opposites in the behavior of the urban population. Furthermore, all of them omit a consideration of most of the routine, everyday, social order that permits a daily reprieve for the dependent millions of the urban islands.

The crisis of the city is thus, in the beginning at least, an intellectual crisis. The inherited images are no longer applicable; they are partial and based upon assumptions about the total society that are unexamined and frequently outmoded. Furthermore, the action crisis of the metropolis cannot be disengaged from the intellectual crisis, for the very definition of a metropolitan problem is dependent upon one's picture of the city and the kind of life it should contain, as the choice of action to improve or revolutionize is dependent upon one's estimate of the city as an existing entity. Those who retain the image of the city as a legal person, a corporate entity, heir to the city-states of Greece, Italy, and medieval Europe, will hardly agree with those who see it chiefly as a spatial sample of a massified society. Their notions of what is, what should be, and how it may be brought about, will tend toward the poles of possibility.

The peculiar quality of this confusion, however, is the presumption of partial validity that each image of the city elicits. While the city is not "militarily autonomous," its corporate nature cannot be dismissed. Anyone who has heard the Viziers of City Hall in a great metropolis refer proudly to "The City" is disabused of the notion. No matter how the rulers are recruited, they control a polity most immediately felt by the citizen, for they rule him "where he lives." Nor can we forget the economic basis of the city and the patterns of land use that order it in space. Where, then, does the failure of urban social science lie? It would be presumptuous to answer with more than hypotheses; however, the statement of such propositions may clarify the problem of improving our image of the city. Implied or stated in the foregoing discussions, three weaknesses in the conceptualization of urban society are baldly evident: the inadequate empirical relevance of many of these images, the partial nature of the approaches, and their limited scope and special nature.

### EMPIRICAL RELEVANCE

The failure of various images of the city to be empirically relevant may not be apparent to the casual reader; our own daily observations are so persuasive as generalities that we unconsciously validate the casual empiricism of the image maker while our own values make it easy to accept the order proffered by our favorite ideologue. Yet, if the foregoing argument has virtue, arbitration among competing images is badly needed. We must cease to think like the supposed object of study, and become the student. For this purpose, the final arbiter of social science must be the empirical argument; such an argument, however, is applicable only when the image itself may be reduced to empirically relevant theory. Failure to do so has been one cause for the multiplication of images.

Some of the images are inherently untestable as stated, for they cannot possibly be falsified. Spengler, Marx, Ortega, each assumes a natural law whose unfolding can never be foretold within the limits of test: it must be inferred after the fact. Further, such ideologues appeal also to natural right, and assume that in the long run the course of history will move toward their own judgment of human behavior. We need not multiply examples of such a position. When, however, these images of the mass society are shorn of their evolutionary presuppositions and their evaluative connotations and used as working guides, they become very different. Discounting the data from the past at the same rate we use for present observations, and eliminating proleptic prediction (or prophecy) as data, we remain with a host of hypotheses as guides to the description of social behavior in the societies and cities of today.

Such description as we have available, however, suffers from sampling bias. The early studies of Gold Coast and slum, as well as very recent reports on the new suburbia, represent a selection of polar extremes and a heightening of dramatic contrasts through uncontrolled inference from limited observation. A theory that emphasizes extremes does not necessarily tell us anything at all about the excluded middle, which may, after all, include the vast majority of urban residents. The wealthy social circles of exurbia, the enclaves of the company men, are latter day equivalents of the "Taxi-Dance Hall" and the "Hobohemia": their use as ideal types of modern urban society is suspect indeed.

Nor can we accept, as clinching evidence in arbitrating among the images, the analysis of mass data provided by the census. It is limited indeed, and there are few postulates constructed to satisfactorily carry the argument from statistical aggregates to the nature of ongoing behavior. The rhetoric of mass statistics tells us, for example, little about the nature of metropolitan government: size, number, variety of suburban municipalities, and similar data have no self-evident connection with the nature of the political process in suburbia. Nor can we infer a great deal from the information that more crime is committed in the metropolis than the middle-sized city, in the slum than in the suburb. Ingenious and skillful analysts continue to order the data provided by the census: it is a distortion of method, leading to a distortion of theory, to presume that such data will have more than a very narrow relevance to such images of the social city as we have adduced.

But the journalist, the shrewd observer, the analyst of census data, has provided most of the evidence for and against the various images of the city. None can, in the nature of his trade, supply the data for a crucial test—none of the images can be "mapped into" a model and evaluated so easily as that.

### THE PARTIALLY EXPLICATED NATURE OF THEORY

A partially explicated theory assumes propositions in its basic explanations that are never made explicit and related to its other aspects; thus, it omits serious consideration of behavior that is crucial even to the limited aspect of things with which it deals. The advocates of scientific management in public administration focus straitly upon the formal machinery, knowing that the party structure and the various kinds of community influence constantly sway behavior away from bureaucratic norms. The urban ecologist ignores the social organization producing spatial patterns as well as that resulting from contiguity or separation. The student of public finance assumes as given, not only the economic history of his metropolis, but the mutual impact of the private enterprises and the public fisc.

To be sure, any approach must abstract; the key question, then, is the determination of criteria for exclusion or inclusion. There are two major guiding notions; first, we must include that which is necessary to the full explication of our theory (the image must be complete); second, we must move toward a closer "fit" between our theory and the delimited aspect of behavior upon which we are focused (the image must be tested). Ideally, all that is included in a given scientific approach, all that constitutes a given image of the city, must be "internal." It must make sense in the same vocabulary. An integrated approach to the urban polity does not adduce psychosomatic medicine, the technology of flood control, and the biology of fecundity into its framework *without translation*.

As the need is felt for further explanation, however, the tendency has been to add theory from every level of explanation, to mix metaphors unmercifully. Consequently, the special cases begin to outnumber the rule and social science becomes a very idiomatic language. Logically, the consequences are fatal: all can be explained after the fact, nothing can be predicted. The *ad hoc* notions from various sources become outriggers that prevent the boat from capsizing, at the cost of getting the boat in the water.

Thus, a major weakness in the various images of the city has been their lack of complete explication, and this results in a very hazy delimitation of explanatory power. The theory that is not delimited as to its application has a tendency to be continually absorbing notions at every level of generality, leaving unanswered the major question of its own internal logic, and therefore the point at which it can be profitably related to other images from other disciplines. In this light, the interdisciplinary tendency in urban studies may be a vitiating influence, for it weakens the integrity of each evolving image without uniting them in an orderly fashion.

### THE LIMITED SCOPE OF URBAN THEORY

However, the images tend more and more to inter-penetrate as the political scientist concerns himself with the economic growth of the city, the ecologist struggles to relate the increasingly important effects of government to the old regularities of land use, and the economist tries to deal with the corporation as a private government, the government as a public enterprise. Such shifts are not due solely to the internal dynamics of each theoretical approach; they are vitally related to the shifting relations between the great institutional areas of the society. Shrewd observers relying on personal observation note that politics may be seen as a "consumption of goods," the customer and firm as a single "organizational system," or the urban area as an "ecology of games." They are mixing their metaphors consciously; the effort is sparked by observation of the changing relations among major areas of the culture.

At the same time, the kaleidoscope of images betrays a wavering and rapidly shifting focus—where are the key structures of the city, and what changes are definitive? Are they located in the metropolitan region as a whole? the mass society? the suburbs? the central city? The spatial abstraction (the "given" image of a congestion of human activity on the face of the earth) is evidently not defining: further and other abstraction is required.

The interpenetration of images and the shifting focus both reflect the over-all dynamics of the carrying society. The analysis of the city that views it as spatially abstracted eliminates (1) the relation between the city and the larger society, and therefore (2) the key dynamics in the evolving society that largely determine the relations between institutional areas and the significant organizational unit for observation. A theory limited to "the city" is too narrow in scope to explain the changing landscape of the city itself.

## The Aim of This Study

If the above analysis is useful, it should provide directives for the reinterpretation of contemporary urban society and the reformulation of the urban image. Such a reinterpretation must have a wider scope, a more specific empirical reference, and a greater theoretical integrity than those discussed above.

It must emphasize the study of the urban complex as a structure, but a structure intimately related to the nature of the carrying society. Thus, the image of the city must be contained within an over-all picture of urban society; "urbanization" and "urbanism," in this approach, become adjectives referring to a society, not merely its population concentrations. Furthermore, such a picture must be congruent with long-term change—in the general society, in the nature of the city, and in the relations between the two.

The approach must yield an empirically relevant image, one that can be tested at many points. It must be based upon the data available, particularly those data free from the limitations of sampling bias and uncontrolled inference. It must, further, yield new vantage points from which to view old problems and create new problems with enough salience to force reconsiderations and improvements in the over-all image.

Finally, it must be guided by a concern for theoretical integrity. The focus must be delimited, the internal structure of the theory must be explicated, otherwise the image is neither clearly applicable nor testable. Consequently, however, all aspects of urban life cannot be considered. Whether those emphasized are the most useful for such an enterprise is a decision that will rest with the arbiters of improved empirical evidence and, finally, the pragmatic test of intellectual history.

# ORDER

# AND CHANGE

# IN

# METROPOLITAN

# SOCIETY

CHAPTER **2**

F WE FORGET the map of America drawn to a scale of statute miles and see only the people and their distribution, we find a nation of mushrooming metropolitan areas, stagnant small towns, and dying open country neighborhoods. Across the countryside the human landscape visibly shifts almost from moment to moment. The farming areas grow increasingly prairie-like as the density of human population dwindles and the size of holding increases; many small towns lose their reason for being, changing to villages and ghost towns;

the small cities become "metropolitan areas" and the great cities expand until they form vast urban regions stretching from Virginia to Maine, from southern Wisconsin to Indiana, and down two hundred miles of California coast.

Thus the process of urban concentration, first dramatically brought to our attention in the President's Report on Recent Social Trends in 1933, has continued to change the shape of the human map.[1] However, the urban agglomerations of the mid-century appear less and less similar to those of the early depression years. Decentralization around the central city, noted in the Report, has continued at such a pace that the diffused, expanding seas of subdivision today blur the very image of the city. Los Angeles County is perhaps atypical in the extremity of its sprawl; the third largest urban concentration of more than six million people spreads over 2,500 square miles, with no center exhibiting the density found in Chicago, Philadelphia, or New York. If Los Angeles is the "city of the future" as some have argued, it is a city of diffusion.

Los Angeles is an extreme case (though we must remember Dallas-Fort Worth, Kansas City, Miami, Phoenix, San Diego, Albuquerque); however, when we look to the growing edges of the other large cities we find a similar case—in Chicago, St. Louis, Atlanta, or Scranton. The changes that we can see at their climax in Los Angeles are typical of mid-twentieth-century urban America. The city disperses, with declining density at the center. The Chicago metropolitan area doubles its population, while the celebrated "loop," the civic center and symbol of urbanism, actually shrinks. Everywhere the center decays and the peripheries boom.

The social allocation of space within the city changes in an equally striking fashion. The elite moves from the mansions of the Gold Coast or Beacon Hill into the rolling hills and ranch houses of suburbia; its place is taken by southern migrants, Negro and white. The central core of the City tends toward a vast ethnic ghetto, surrounding the "white lights" and surrounded, in turn, by miles of residential streets of a shabby gentility whose residents consider the approach of the Puerto Ricans, the Negroes, the Mexicans, or the Okies. Meanwhile, back in the suburbs, the flood of new migrants from the central city and outside the metropolitan area is increasingly composed of the vast middle range of urban people. Suburbia no longer stands for the well-to-do, but rather for the scale from "decent home-owning people" up to the millionaires. The key question is not city or suburb, but which suburb? For suburbia becomes, increasingly, the sum of neighborhoods that once comprised most of the central city.

This reordering in space accompanies other important changes. The average man of today's metropolis differs greatly from his counterpart of earlier decades. While the population is shifting in the nation, and the neighborhoods within the metropolis change their character, the entire social system of the metropolitan complex is in movement. It is useful to consider three separate dimensions of change along which it is traveling, dimensions by which we can order and compare different neighborhoods of the metropolis, and also differing cities—or the same city at different points in time. They are social rank, life style, and ethnicity. Social rank indicates the "objective" factors of social class: occupation, education, income. Life style refers to the way of life chosen by the population—whether the family-committed life of the suburbs, or the life of the working couple in the apartment-house areas of the city. Ethnicity refers to the differentiation of the population by racial and cultural background—the proportion and kinds of minority groups to be found in the neighborhood, or the city.[2]

Using each attribute as an index, we find that contemporary American urban populations are in a process of lively change. Social rank moves steadily upward: the population increasingly has had a high school education, has a job level higher than that of the unskilled laborer, and a real income much greater than that of the previous generation. At the same time, the life style of metropolitan populations considered as a whole have changed in the direction of an increasing emphasis upon home and family. Fewer women choose a childless career; fertility rates soar, passing those of such nations as Russia and India. Most new residential building is of the single-family type. Finally, with the closing of gates on immigration, the great populations of native Italians, Poles, Russians, Jews, and others from southern and eastern Europe are rapidly dying out. The foreign-born decline with each census and their children are grandparents, living in the suburbs as often as in the central city. In their place, however, the Puerto Ricans, Mexicans, Negroes, and "hillbillies" from the South enter in response to the demand for heavy labor. Thus, the older ethnic enclaves become harder to identify and of less importance in differentiating the cultural and social life of the city, while the segregated populations in the central core become increasingly dark in color, and more difficult to promote into the majority.

In summary, there are basic changes occurring in the

rural-urban balance of the nation, in the composition of the metropolitan complex as a whole, and in the characteristics of the various subareas and neighborhoods within each urban area. On the surface, the metropolitan society is heterogeneous, its patterns transitory. Any effort to discover the basis of order must, then, account for change—and change must be explained in terms of basic structural conditions. In describing such conditions we must consider the very nature of urbanization itself.

## Urbanization and the Scale of a Society

The emphasis upon describing the concentration of population in urban centers during the past three centuries has sometimes distracted attention from the more basic question: what is happening to a society that makes possible, if not mandatory, this concentration of population? Today, as various observers question the primacy of the older city and foresee a much greater deconcentration of population than we are already witnessing, it seems useful to conceive of urbanization, not as simply the multiplication of old-style cities, but as a characteristic of a total society. It is a characteristic that might better be described as *an increase in societal scale*.[3] The trends in the larger society may, then, make possible a reasonable explanation of the changes in given metropolitan areas. We shall proceed through a brief description of the city as a social structure, a discussion of the dynamics of increase in scale, and, finally, a consideration of the relations between these dynamics and the changing structure of the city.

THE STATICS OF THE CITY

A city is a vast and striking example of what we mean by the phrase, "a geographical division of labor."[4] The urban concentration is possible only because the basic extractive activities of field, forest, fishery and mine allow the maintenance of a large population having little access to the productive earth; further, the urban concentration processes and produces goods and services that are the basis of exchange with the hinterland. Most important, the urban center produces the over-all ordering of societal activities—its most crucial export is control. The market mechanism centers in cities; the formal agencies of government are urban in their situation; the organizations that process and diffuse meaning are largely urban—the mass media, the churches, a large proportion of the publishing houses and universities. Economic, political, ecclesiastical, and symbolic control center overwhelmingly in the city. This is the sense in which order may be considered the defining product of the city within the division of labor embracing the total society.[5]

This means that, today, in certain places *and no other* the functional centers of control in the society are located. Here are found a large proportion of the population, the overwhelming concentration of fluid wealth, and the processes of cultural innovation and formulation that take place in American society. Within the metropolitan area, however, geographical distribution is an important set of limits and clues to order. The map of the metropolis may be drawn to indicate the division of labor and the division of rewards among the population.

The division of labor is manifest in the different uses

to which various parts of the land area are allocated. Influencing this pattern from the beginning are the transportation media—the routes of wagon trains or the ports for helicopters.[6] Toward the center, where exchange is easiest, lie the governmental agencies, the financial and securities markets, the offices of corporations, and the merchants who must draw their market from a large population: these facilities make up the downtown; they cluster at the crossing of transportation routes. The industrial plant lies between market and transportation and is central to the population that supplies its labor force. The merchants whose goods are in demand from all alike locate in a dispersed pattern throughout the city.

The division of labor among the population is also reflected in the division of rewards, and one of the most important rewards in our society is the dwelling place. The cost of the dwelling in income and in time and expense of the journey to work is closely related to the job. Thus the nature of a residential neighborhood in physical terms is related closely to the residents' share in the economic surplus, in social honor, and in the symbolic surplus or "culture" of the society.[7] To the broad categories of land use reflecting the division of labor in the metropolis we must add the broad categories of residential neighborhoods, reflecting the division of rewards.

The metropolitan area in this perspective is highly differentiated, including a great variety of land uses and, within the category of residential use, a great variety of neighborhoods. However, these various populations are not only allocated different geographical subareas for their residential neighborhoods and workplaces, corresponding to their roles in the division of labor—they are also integrated within common schemes of action. Their interdependence may be gauged by the impossibility of survival for any particular part of the metropolis in isolation, while the interdependence of city and total society is equally clear. No individual in the city, no social class, can survive without the rights it can claim from others; these rights in turn stem from the functions allocated to the individual within the total complex.

What are the mechanisms of integration? The greater the differentiation of social roles, the greater must be the interdependence among a population. How then is this dispersed population, to which many and diverse activities are allocated, integrated into a working system of activity and exchange with a high degree of predictability? How do those who produce "one-eighteenth of a pin" cooperate to produce entire pins, and exchange pins alone for the entire physical necessities of life?

The mechanisms upon which integration must rely are the social groups that, based upon the interdependence of many actors, coordinate their behavior through the flow of communication.[8] A group, as the term is used here, does not simply refer to any aggregation of people. It refers to an aggregation existing in a state of interdependence, with a stable flow of communication and a consequent ordering of behavior. Thus, the group is a structure among individuals; its members may change while it persists—and it may disappear, though its members continue to exist in other group structures. Furthermore, a group must not be reified—no single group controls all of any person's actions, and some control very little. The bounds of a group are determined by the compliance of individuals with their duties, as defined by the role system and the normative order of the group. One must, then, approach a social group through the aggregation, not through the single person. In studying the organizational structure of the city we must translate the uniform behavior, the patterns persisting through time (whether of land use or of police methods) into the vocabulary of group analysis.

The groups that make up the organizational system of a city may be classified in many ways; for the immediate purpose, the most important distinction is that between exclusive *membership* groups, and inclusive *spatial* groups. Exclusive membership groups range in size from giant corporations to friendship cliques, and their tasks vary in a comparable fashion; inclusive groups may be as small as a neighborhood, as large as London, with a comparable variation in size and complexity. The major difference is that the tasks of the exclusive membership group have no necessary, inescapable base in a specific area; those of the inclusive spatial group are all generated by the condition of its defining area.

The exclusive membership group, whether a sewing circle or a manufacturing concern, has specific criteria for entrance and therefore selects from the total population in an area. Spatially undefined, it may include few, none, or all of those in a given neighborhood, and it may straddle geographical areas that are widely separated. Thus, it is possible for many groups of the same kind to exist in the same geographical area, in isolation from each other, in competition, conflict, or collusion. Such groups represent, at most, only some of the population in a given space. The spatially inclusive group, however, includes all those active in its defined area, and only those; it is geographically inclusive and exclusive, hence, spatially defined. It may control, however, only a small segment of its members' behavior (they must pay their water bill to the district), and may, therefore, compete with other spatially defined groups. Such groups represent segments of the behavior of *all the persons committed to a given geographical area.*

Membership groups rest upon an interdependence that may be easily identified, for it is the product of this interdependence that constitutes the sanctions controlling behavior. The economic corporation can control behavior through the pay check, for this is the functional basis of its existence; in the friendship clique, people are "cut off," through ostracism, criticism, ridicule. These groups may be imagined as simple circular systems: they have access to a certain amount of energy that is processed through the internal work, the social order of the group, and that produces enough "output" to insure their access to another supply of energy. The corporation requires raw materials, processes them, and through the market can purchase raw materials anew. The friendship clique requires the time and energy of members, produces from these a "social surplus" (the social process or interaction as a value in itself) and can, therefore, purchase future time from its members.[9]

From this analysis, it is apparent that the ongoing structure of the exclusive membership group requires both an internal order and a predictable relationship with its external environment. "Problems" can arise at either point; those deriving from the group's "foreign relations" are crucial to this discussion of the spatially inclusive group. Although membership groups have comparative freedom of location, they nevertheless must settle somewhere. The inescapable localization of their activities means that (1) they automatically have neighbors, and (2) they are within the borders of an inclusive spatial group. Those who see the city as "nature's half acre" emphasize this necessary contiguity of the most diverse group structures; they assume a very minimal order—for obviously the kind of order possible within an exclusive membership group is difficult to imagine for a sample of the earth's surface containing households, corporations, cliques, political groups and football teams in proximity.[10]

However, much more order than the blind ecological interplay of forces is demanded in the cramped quarters of the city. In the first place, sheer contiguity of action creates, from overlapping sites, a common interest in the over-all scene. Air pollution, water pollution, organized violence, fire danger, may be produced outside the group —but may present a major menace to its activity. Other groups become possible barriers to the performance of any group's tasks. In the second place, contiguous groups become necessary conditions for others' existence, as in the case of the corporation's dependence on newspaper advertisements, or the urban household's dependence upon both. Finally, certain necessary facilities are allocated only to the spatially defined group in our society: the streets, sewers, parks, and public docks, are major bases for interdependence among diverse groups within the city.

The city itself may be conceived as one macroscopic role system, in which categories of groups perform the various tasks necessary for the totality to stay alive and healthy in the conditions of interdependence. (Such tasks correspond to what some call "functions.") Each category of group has rights and duties, has its charter so to speak

—and there are over-all norms that apply to all groups. These are formalized in the law. And municipal government, overshadowed in some ways by the nation-state, is still the mediator and the enforcer. The housekeeping problems arising from contiguity, from the very density of interdependent organizations, demand an over-all group within which the roles are assigned to corporate persons.

Thus, the division of labor in the city is integrated through the orders internal to the exclusive organizations, through the order between them (whether of market or of law), and through norms applying to all citizens of the city. The media through which organization proceeds, in turn, are the communications systems, which allow the movement of information, influence, and orders, and the transportation system, which allows the movement of energy in the form of persons and goods. No physical aspect of the city is more crucial than these media: they make possible combination of the heterogeneous activities of heterogeneous populations scattered over space. They permit one group's "output" to be another's "input." They allow the complex social structure of the city to perpetuate itself, setting limits upon integration; when they change those limits change.

Such are the bare bones of the city; a division of labor distributed over space, associated with a division of rewards that, in the form of residence, is also spatially distributed, coordinated through organizational structures that produce and depend upon the flow of messages, persons, and goods. The integration of the city is only a particular case of the integration of any social system; it is based upon a network of interdependence and a resulting "mutual modification of behavior," extending over space and through time.

# The Dynamics of Increase in Scale

The dynamics of metropolitan society are implicit in the basic structure presented; if we wish to understand the important changes going on in the metropolis, we must look to the societal changes in the geographical division of labor and in the processes of integration. Doing so, we find concurrent trends in both, mutually dependent, their interaction producing very rapid shifts in the carrying society and in its relations with the city.

If we take, as a beginning, American industry in the mid-nineteenth century, the most striking changes since have been (1) the increasing use of nonhuman sources of energy, translated through machines into human values; (2) the increasing span of the organizational networks in which men and machines are integrated for productive and distributive purposes; and (3) a resulting increase in the amount of productivity for each human participant.

The increasing rate of energy transformation includes greatly improved transportation and communication media; the consequences may be summarized in one statement— the space-time ratio (or cost in time for traveling a given distance) has greatly decreased. This is apparent in the transportation of persons and goods (including energy, such as electricity) and in the transmission of messages. The implications of these changes are that space, for all practical purposes, is no longer fixed. It is a barrier to the extension of activities, but as the mechanisms of extension improve it becomes simply a channel for integration. Thus, the shrinking space-time ratio allows the use of human actors who are increasingly widely separated but whose activities can be just as closely coordinated as before.[11]

This makes possible the increased span of organizational networks that coordinate behavior. Geographical division of labor includes intensive agricultural specialization, with an increased emphasis upon the national market and decline of the subsistence aspect of farming, and a similar development of industrial and service specialization. Recreation is increasingly a function centered in two cities, with the entire nation dependent upon them— just as it depends upon the Texas gas deposits for heat, the Florida and California groves for morning citrus. Such extreme specialization can only be coordinated through giant organizations, rapid transport, and a national market where information is exchanged at the speed of electric currents or radio waves.

The increased use of nonhuman energy and machinery, however, has also produced a rapid shift in the distribution of the labor force. Agricultural and other extractive industries demand a smaller proportion of the total; manufacturing also demands only a small proportion (though production increases rapidly) and the proportion in the professional, clerical, and service occupations increases steadily. Complex machinery using nonhuman energy increases the proliferation of occupational classes. There are greater demands for highly skilled labor as the unskilled laborer ceases to be the base for the industrial pyramid (his place taken by the machine). At the same time, the growth of the large-scale control systems, the bureaucracies of business and government, increases the proportion of workers whose job is in the making, processing, and distribution of messages—that is, order and control. Thus, the primary orientation of many workers is toward either complex symbolic problems or people, and this in turn leads to higher formal educational qualifications. Finally, changes in the organization of work cause an increase in productivity per person, and a steady upward movement of the average rewards.

Thus, as the society increases in scale, only a small and dwindling proportion remain rural, and there is a general upward movement of the entire population with respect to occupational level, educational level, and income level. Occupations require more learning of the society's symbolic store and more individual discrimination; they yield more rewards in the form of leisure, access to goods and services, and (with higher education) access to meaning, or "culture." Altogether, the societal surplus in man-hours, money, and symbols, spells a very wide latitude of choice for the average individual, compared with any previous historical epoch.[12]

### INCREASE IN SCALE: THE NATIONAL SYSTEM

The process of increase in societal scale is a vast, complex, and completely interdependent process. The consequences of the process are revolutionary for human life; they change the nature of the human home in society to a form it has never before manifested. While material technologies have been crucial in this development, our chief focus of interest will be upon the equally crucial organizational technologies, those developing forms that have made possible the rational coordination of human activities over vast areas of space and time.

By society we mean the bounded network of interdependence resulting in mutual control of behavior; as the scale of an organizational network increases, so does the

meaningfully defined "society." Increase in scale, however, includes both an extension of the society and a transformation of the internal order. The extension of the
control system may be initiated by either military force
or trade, resulting in the dominance of either the governmental or the economic system, but they tend eventually
to coincide in scale, for the two kinds of order are com-
plementary. Government sets the rules within which economic exchange can develop, while economic exchange
demands such rules. However originated, the process knits
together diverse populations into a single network of interdependence; through migration toward the centers of surplus, through amalgamation into a larger governmental and
economic unit, the constituent populations are conjoined.
Their ethnic histories differentiate them one from another,
but their dependence, their communication and their tasks
subject them to the influence of the "moving total" that
makes up the society of increasing scale.

At the societal level, looking from the center of the
organizational network, the extension of the control systems has three aspects of major importance: (1) the widening of the radii of interdependence, (2) the increasing
range of the communications flow, and (3) the widening
span of control and compliance.

1. *The widening of the radii of interdependence means
that, whether men know it or not, they become mutual
means to individual ends.* As mutual dependence is translated into social relations and these become organizations,
control centers arise for the purpose of relating the various
activities of each extended organization and, equally important, the relationships among various organizations. His-
torically, such control centers have been in cities, whether

the control is economic, political, or ecclesiastical. The importance of the city for the surrounding society is then necessarily a function of the extensiveness and the intensity of interdependence. We have spoken of the transformation of the internal order of a society with increase in scale; this transformation results, in part, from the increasing number of necessary societal tasks that are delegated to large, specialized organizational networks. As the basic tasks so ordered increase in number, the *intensity of interdependence* increases. The society of the tenth century in Europe moved toward large-scale integration of religious control, but this was not accompanied by political and economic control. Consequently, the control centers, the "cities" of the bishoprics, were of comparatively small account in ordering the entire range of the behavior of the European population. Their growth into the cities of contemporary Europe reflects, as Pirenne makes clear, the increase in the intensity of interdependence, or, as Shevky and Bell phrase it, "the increase in the range of activities centered in cities."[13]

Thus the growth of cities is a direct result (and a reinforcing mechanism) of the increase in scale of carrying societies. Though specific societies manifest varying causal sequences, and the city or the state may have been at a given point a "prime mover" toward the next stage of expansion, cities are dependent for their existence upon their role as control centers in the large-scale market, government, ecclesia, or some combination of such structures. Typically, contemporary cities are headquarters or subsidiary centers of the national market and the nation state.

2. *As a concomitant of the widening radii of interdependence, increasing scale produces an increasing range*

*and content of the communications flow.* That is, communication from a given center goes further and affects more people in more ways. Communication is a vital part of the organizational structures that integrate action; as interdependence increases in scope, then, increased communication is a necessary condition for handling the problems it poses. Inadequate communications (whether of persons, goods, or messages) will, in fact, prevent the translation of interdependence into organization (thus the media of communication severely limited the possible scale of the early empires.)[14] The tendency toward increase in scale may be accelerated by improved communication. It may also be checked or reversed through communications failures, for the vital structural members, the extended organizations to which are delegated basic societal tasks, may be unable to perform at a minimal level.

The large-scale organizational networks are instrumental in carrying the communications flow of the larger society. The corporation, state bureaucracy, or bureaucracies of church, labor union and voluntary organizations, are basically oriented to their own survival and housekeeping needs. But they also carry a diverse content of messages and symbols through the relevant populations, by-products irrelevant to the carrying organization, from jokes to propaganda. And, at the same time, communication becomes itself a specialized network of formal organizations, for it becomes a social product with exchange value at the marketplace. The mass-media industries arise, allowing a form of direct communication with a very large proportion of the total population that bypasses organizational structures.

The centers of the communications networks—whether

of the formal organizational systems or of the mass media themselves—are typically situated in cities. They carry messages that are delivered from the point of view of those who sit on a high place and see far, those who live at the center among the "peak organizations" of modern man. They become impregnated with urban norms they then diffuse, directly and indirectly, to the total society. In this sense the city is a prime mover—not because it is a large, dense, heterogeneous collection of nonagricultural persons—but because it is at the control and communications center of the total society. It "acculturates" the total society to a new point of view. Much of what we have called urbanism is subsumed under this point of view, but when it becomes diffused throughout a society, what shall we call it? It implies wider horizons, larger scale, a frame of reference that is societal rather than local. It is, essentially, cosmopolitanism, the way of life in the great polity.

3. *The increase in scale results in a widening span of compliance and control with given social organizations.* The necessities of persistence, when interdependence is so widespread, lead to a constant increase in the size and functions of specific organized groups. Corporations, labor unions, governmental bureaus, churches, whose members become private (or semipublic) governments are, with their dependents, major proportions of the total population. Such organizations are relatively free of a given locality; they are exclusive membership groups that span cities, counties, and states, but that control only their immediate members and publics.

These organizations manifest certain structural similarities, due to the necessary conditions of specialization and integration. They are, first of all, enormous systems

within which the key actors are employees. They manifest a complex division of labor, a proliferation of roles
and formalized norms of interaction. They are hierarchi-
cally organized, with great variations in the power and
the rewards available to actors in the different scalar roles.
They emphasize particularly the importance of technical
and organizational specialists: those who control symbols
and people are their elites. They are, in short, bureaucracies.

The salience of such large-scale organizations in the
society, their nationwide span of control, and the similarity of their division of labor and rewards, tend to develop a stratification system cutting across widely varying
geographical and cultural subregions of the society. The
system is based upon function, translated into occupational
classification and the associated rewards. It is indifferent
to, if not antithetical to, older stratification systems based
upon origin—"social class" in Warner's sense, or "race."[15]
Such role systems are oriented toward a national organization, a nation-wide industry, a nation-wide profession,
rather than the conventions of the particular *locale* in
which they find themselves. Though the members may
reside in the hinterland, their true home is still the organizational networks, their hallowed ground the headquarters
city. They are representatives of a corporate society, like
the member of the Society of Jesus or the colonial officer
in the jungle.

They are national citizens.

INCREASE IN SCALE: THE LOCALITY GROUP

From the point of view of the analyst concerned with
organizational systems, the process of increase in scale is

one that involves scattered and distinctive subgroups in a larger order. Within this expanding order they either assume corporate roles or disintegrate, their actors being assigned roles in the larger system. In either case, the local group becomes dependent upon, then interdependent with, the expanding network of activity. This is accompanied by an increase in the amount of communication flow and its range, and results in the acculturation of the interdependent populations to a normative structure that assumes and implements the larger system. With increasing compliance of the locality group's members, an ordering of behavior results that is nation-wide in scope. Much of what is called "urbanization" (the concentration of population in cities) may be interpreted as increasing interdependence; that which is termed "urbanism" reflects the acculturation of subgroups to a society-wide normative structure; the phenomena sometimes referred to as "conformism" or "uniformity" (or "loss of individualism") may be interpreted as compliance with the norms of large scale organizations, spanning the society.

When one turns his attention to any specific subgroups within the total society (locality group, village, ethnic enclave, or colony) the process is reciprocated in (1) loss of autonomy, (2) exposure to conflicting norms, and (3) fragmentation of the total social order.[16]

1. *The loss of autonomy* is inevitable, for as the local group is integrated in a larger order the price is loss of economic and governmental self-sufficiency. The extended but exclusive membership organizations become crucial to the ongoing of the local area (providing resources, protection, transportation, and the like) yet their control centers are far away. These organizations are specialized

and do not include all of the spatially defined group; at the same time they include members from many scattered localities. As functions are transferred to such organizations, people become less dependent on the near at hand, and the local group's *raison d'être* in autonomy is considerably weakened.

2. *Exposure to conflicting norms* from afar, through the organizational networks or the mass media, is a major result. Members are exposed, outside the surveillance and control of the local community, to wider horizons, to norms and models not immediately given in their social environment. The loss of cultural *apartheid* would be, in any case, a problem for the existing local normative order. Since the new messages are brought through the channels of the larger, dominant society, however, they are a direct threat to the unique norms and values evolved in the local group.

3. *Fragmentation of the local normative order* is a predictable consequence; some of the members of the local group must conform to patterns from afar, since they are dependent upon the large, extended organization for their livelihood. Others take advantage of the local group's loss of coercive power to exploit added degrees of freedom; they experiment with new means to old ends, they try new ends, they exercise freedom of choice. Others, still, are dependent upon the local order for social position and rewards; their life is controlled by its norms, but with the attrition of dependence (and therefore the basis for order), they find it impossible to communicate or to enforce compliance. (The cutting edge of the sanctions depended, after all, upon the interdependence of the local group.) When individuals become committed to groups centering out-

side the locality, the new dependence brings a measure of independence from their neighbors.

Thus the local group loses its integrity and approaches amalgamation in the large-scale society. The behavior of its members in many crucial areas of activity cannot be understood, save as a part of the role system in the nation-wide corporation, labor union, political party, or governmental bureau. *Social* amalgamation is evident in the dominance of local action by the extended organization. Acculturation is equally obvious, as the ends and means, the "blueprints for living," are changed in the direction of the "urbane"—the society-wide culture.

### INCREASE IN SCALE:
### AUTONOMY AND CENTRALIZATION

The argument thus far leads to the conclusion that when a society increases in scale it experiences an initial increase in differentiation, becoming in many matters poly-glot and conflict ridden, a "mosiac of worlds that touch but do not interpenetrate." However, as the process continues, the society moves toward cultural homogeneity and conformity to the larger order: "urbanism" eventually accompanies compliance. The argument, pushed to its logical conclusion, may result in images of "the mass society" leading, in turn, to robot citizens and the totalitarian state. It certainly indicates a diminution of the variety and color derived from ethnic inheritance (whether the origin was in migration, as commonly occurred in the United States, or in peasant societies of the hinterland, as was the case in Europe); it also indicates a decline in the resisting power of the local units.[17]

The decline of the ethnically distinct, organizationally

autonomous locality group does not, however, indicate that such a centralized society is apt to occur. The locality group, village, or metropolis, is an inescapable social form with powerful bases in interdependence. We have noted earlier, in analyzing the structure of the city, the major consequences of the organization's immediate environment. Spatial collocation produces problems of order and a need for common facilities, strengthening the local role system and resulting in a coercive power over the actions of each exclusive membership group. The corporation or state bureaucracy must come to earth in order to work, and wherever it does it finds neighbors.

It also tends to take root. We have emphasized the functional basis of the large-scale bureaucracies in the *social product*: they provide sustenance, protection, social honor—products instrumental to the various ends of their members. We must remember that a given group may also have, as its functional basis, the *social process*—or interaction as a valued end in itself. The social process is very apt to emerge in any group; once present, it affects the strength of the group, for it increases interdependence, extends and enriches the normative structure and the role system, and makes possible a very rigorous control over the behavior of the constituent members.

The social process is the basis for that aspect of social structure that Cooley calls the "primary group."[18] Such is its power that some analysts have equated it with necessary conditions for personality organization and security; certainly it humanizes the environment, calling out many bases for loyalty and devotion other than the overt function of the group—the social product. It is most apt to arise in face-to-face interaction, among small aggregates that, for whatever reason, interact repeatedly and often. Therefore, the local setting of the organization has a strong tendency to foster local commitments. In friendship pairs, cliques, and fraternities, (and sometimes even a "community" including all members of the spatially defined group) the social process results in commitments to the normative structure of the spatially inclusive group, vulnerability to its sanctions and compliance with its rules.

For these reasons the local "branches" of large-scale organizations are not immune to the normative order of the locality group. Their tasks force them to take account of the neighbors, and their involvement in primary group relations leads to a two-way traffic in influence. Another consequence of the primary dimension, one that has been often noted (though chiefly as a problem internal to the large-scale bureaucracy) is the likelihood that the local group in the organization will itself develop a powerful primary dimension—one separating "this branch" from the remainder of "the organization." Such localism, when accompanied by tendencies toward variations in norms and roles (the inevitable result of specific application from general rules), may result in a distinct subculture within the firm or agency—and this subculture is apt to persist because of its organizational base. Such a subculture will often incorporate many of the norms of the locality group within which the branch is located. This is especially likely if members are recruited from local boys, but, even with recruitment from distant localities, primary relationships with necessary associates make the exclusive organization permeable to its cultural and its organizational surroundings.

As a result, there is a general tension between the large-scale, segmentally defined, formal organization on one hand, and the small-scale nuclear groups that make up its task forces. The latter must commit themselves, in some degree, to the normative order of the locality group—they are dependent upon it in carrying out the very tasks assigned by the larger system. Furthermore, spatial separation from the larger structure and spatial segregation (along with members of many other groups) in a given locale, tend to produce in some matters greater differences *between* spatially separated groups than *within* each group considered separately. The increasing acculturation of the society to metropolitan scale does not, then, result only in a tendency toward standardization. Differentiation is created anew, by the ancient mechanisms of *relative isolation* and *differential association* among those in a given spatial area as compared with those scattered afar.

## Integration That Knits the Map

Though the city is no longer an island of urban settlement in a sea of feudal agrarians, with walls symbolizing its military autonomy and a government coterminous with its population, it is still an organizational unit. The highly differentiated set of activities necessary for its persistence require complex and effective integrative mechanisms in order to produce predictability and structural stability through time, for the city displays massive uniformities, orderly change, remarkable stability. The burden upon these mechanisms can be appreciated when we consider the pandemonium resulting in cities that experience catastrophe. And the everyday activities required to perpetuate the system are staggering in their complexity and order: each day the food and water for biological persistence, the resources for work, the market mechanism that allocates values, operate with a high degree of precision—and the city is fed.

The basic tasks are accomplished through a series of organized groups. Ranging in size from the household to the corporation, these may be differentiated and grouped by the essential functions they perform. Taken together, those groups performing a given task represent a *functional segment* of the society. Each is an organizational network in which behavior is designed and ordered through an *institutional area* of the culture. The culturally prescribed norms are working patterns, and sanctions based upon the interdependence of individuals and groups serve to give them social affect. The functional segments evolve through time as the inherited culture interacts with changing organizational necessities. As the society increases in scale, the major functional segments ordering work, education, recreation, and other activities become separated out, specialized, and formalized. These segments are increasingly dominated by bureaucracies that fuse through organizational absorptions and expansions into cartels of one sort or another. Still other societal tasks remain the prerogative of smaller groups, cliques, play groups, neighborhood, and, most important, the conjugal family. Like the giant corporation, such groups may be analyzed in a framework that begins with the basis of interdependence, derives the role structure and the normative order from this basis, and indicates the sanctions that order behavior.

Thus, much of the behavior of the urban population can be understood and predicted through a knowledge of the group structures that absorb the energy of individuals and coordinate their behavior in time. These same groups also result in the variety of social products and their distribution. Within groups the individual has a specific role, a job to perform; he has rights and duties, and his behavior is ordered by that of persons playing reciprocal roles—those for whom the individual's rights become duties, and vice versa. His behavior is also ordered by norms applying equally to all in the group and for whom all persons become role reciprocals (or enforcers, through informal or formal sanctions) of the group's normative structure.

### INTERSTICES AND THE PROBLEM OF ORDER

Order *within* the organized groups, however, does not necessarily result in over-all order within the metropolis—one bureaucracy or family may create an internal order that only accentuates the lack of integration between the various groups. What is the basis of order between organizations? How do family and school, government and business enterprise, peer group and police relate? Interrelations among groups are problems of order that most organizational analysis, focusing upon the order internal to a group in isolation, cannot answer. Nor do the bureaucratic orders apply to the behavior of the population that takes place outside *any* tightly organized group. Yet much of the urban citizen's time is spent in public places—markets, parks, sidewalks and streets, and places of public entertainment. Here there may be, in some sense, "norms," but who are the reciprocal role players—who enforces the norms?

SOCIAL ORDER: INTERGROUP RELATIONS

The functional segments have their relatively autonomous organizational networks—through the market, economic control, federations, coalitions, and other organizational forms. However, in the concrete and exclusive enterprises that form the task forces of any society, we see a congeries of units whose maintenance of orderly and predictable relations with each other and the joint environment is by no means inevitable. Yet there is a basic and inescapable interdependence among concrete groups who are neighbors within the same urban complex. They are possible blocs to the orderly performance of other groups' tasks—as in the slaughterhouse or chemical plant that is located in a residential area. They are necessary conditions for the maintenance of the work-flow in other groups through provision of resources or markets—as in the relationship between family and school, of business firm and local union. They are necessary partners in common enterprises—as in the maintenance of streets and waste disposal facilities. Consequently, there are many transactions among them, and these must be carried on at a minimal level of order (there must be predictability) if the city is to survive.

This order within the locality group, or local social system, depends upon a communications flow in which the constituent groups have something approaching "roles" —reciprocal rights and duties. These roles reflect the societal allocations of tasks and the means that are legitimate for their performance. They are definitions shared, to some degree, by the controlling personnel in each group. These actors share past organizational experience in the larger society as well as acculturation through the mass media, and each organization's role system includes the problems of dealing with foreign relations.[19] At the same time, these roles or quasi-roles are formalized in the law, which provides social categories within which groups as "legal persons" have specific rights and duties.

When interaction among organizations occurs, then, there is ordinarily an existing set of norms, a crude role system providing a vocabulary for communication among the groups. Such communication is not effective unless sanctions are possible, and sanctions are ordinarily based upon the interdependence of the groups. Such sanctions may be based upon the inevitable commitment of each group to the other, where a close interdependence holds— as in the independent union and the small firm. More frequently, however, we note interdependence that holds between a concrete group and any one of a *class* of other groups—as between a union and hundreds of firms, or a grammar school and hundreds of families. Here the sanctions are less a function of specific, constant role reciprocals, and more often a function of enforcers, who speak and act for a normative order that is general to the classes of groups. Such enforcers may speak for a private, segmental, and autonomous normative order. For example, the Central Labor Council or the Merchants and Manufacturer's Association, may discipline its members who "get out of line" and so, in its way, may the PTA discipline its constituent families.

Another and basic normative system lies within the wider framework of the public law where the legal officials are, in this sense, surrogate role reciprocals. They stand for the relevant "other" whose rights are being violated when the specific group does not perform its duties.

Thus the assigned roles, or social categories, of concrete social groups are maintained through a flow of communication among groups—but frequently an important third party intervenes in the form of the enforcer, who rewards and penalizes in terms of a system applicable to all members in a given spatially inclusive group. The corporate role system depends for immediate sanction upon the locality group—the urban polity.

SOCIAL ORDER: AGGREGATIVE SITUATIONS

A second major type of "extragroup" interaction in the city is that which occurs in aggregate situations, on social sites where all or most of the actors do not form a social group, but are nevertheless in close proximity. Places of public service, such as the market, public parks and squares, and public assemblies, are sites for such aggregates. Others occur in the channels of circulation, where a transient and unorganized aggregate of many types of persons continually occurs. The streets, public transportation, sidewalks, lobbies, and terminals produce "the crowd."

Such collocations of organizationally unrelated persons on a given scene produce inherent interdependence. Other persons are possible barriers and threats to any given individual, for without group support and without a common role system and set of sanctions, the individual is extremely vulnerable. (Some indication of this vulnerability is evident in the occasional remarkable success of youth groups in terrorizing samples of adults considerably more powerful in the aggregate, on the downtown streets of any large city.) Thus the problems of public order are inevitable consequences of urban agglomeration.

Here again the locality group has developed a normative order based upon assigned social categories and generalized norms, or rights. This order cannot be enforced by either the "role reciprocal" or the private enforcer—for dependence is hardly balanced by interdependence. The "hue and cry" is notoriously inefficient in a contemporary metropolis as is the citizen's arrest, and neither has been seriously considered as a mechanism for sanctions for a long time. Instead, the city has developed a characteristically urban role—that of the police. In aggregate situations where there are no constant role reciprocals, where the passerby and the innocent bystander are the only enforcers, the officer of the police is the surrogate role reciprocal. He stands for the norms and must provide the surveillance and enforce the sanctions that maintain the rights and the duties of the passersby.

The task of the policeman would be, however, impossible were there not a high degree of uniformity in the behavior of the crowds. Here we must note the reciprocity in acculturation to the social order of the city on one hand, the total large-scale society on the other. The sanctity of the public order, detached from any given concrete group and personified in the police, is an important message of the mass media. Its analogue is found in the bureaucracies within which the individual lives so much of his life, from the kindergarten to the corporation. Habitual behavior is standardized for aggregate situations, and the enforcers can use the strategy of watching only for the deviant cases.

LOCALITY GROUPS AND THE LARGE-SCALE SOCIETY:
THE CITY AS POLITY

The large-scale society must still maintain a complex social order at the level of the locality. Intergroup relations and aggregate situations emphasize the importance of collocation in space. Private governments specific to the city order many relationships among groups, and the role system within which groups are actors makes possible the integration of allocated tasks. But these, as we note, depend for sanctions upon the legal structure. So do the norms that order the inescapable aggregate behavior of urban populations. This legal structure is in many ways specific to the locality area; the city as a social congeries is dependent upon the city as a polity for its minimal working conditions.

The polity of the city is a summary of the public decisions that can be enforced by legal sanctions. The city changes through time, and as its tasks change there is a corresponding adaptation of the norms and their enforcement. Upon the changing polity are dependent affairs ranging from the maintenance of public order and safety to the physical map of the city. The balance of power among concrete groups in competition or conflict, the nature of public enterprises and the assignment of their costs and benefits are determined within the arena of the policy-forming agencies in the city.

Yet the contemporary city as a governmental structure does not include within its jurisdiction the total population dependent upon the order that local polity must provide. The expanding governmental jurisdiction of the city stopped around the second decade of the twentieth century, in one metropolitan area after another—while expansion continued at the peripheries. Thus the interdependent populations were divided into separate governments—a very large population in the old central city, and a suburban congeries of small municipalities. In consequence,

there is a wide discrepancy between the legal city's electorate and its clients, its allocated tasks and its legal rights.

The governmental decentralization of the city manifest
in suburban municipalities is not, like the decentralization
of production and distribution, integrated within an over-
all system such as the corporation or the local market.
Each municipality has a high degree of autonomy, and to
it are assigned the major tasks spelled out in the preceding
discussion. Some of these tasks may be performed within
such a governmental division of labor—public order in the
suburbs can be maintained, for the suburban populations
are those most uniformly acculturated to the normative
system of the larger society, and the residential nature of
land use obviates most of the anonymous aggregates who
assemble at different points in the central city. Other tasks
are performed through various mechanisms that integrate
the city and the suburbs or integrate a set of suburban
municipalities—contractual arrangements, informal working agreements, and special district governments to which
are allocated a single function such as fire protection.

Some functions cannot, in their nature, be carried out
in such a system. The ordering of relationships among
organized groups cannot be achieved within a spatially defined system when the groups are located in different juris-
dictions. Though much of this order is produced by private
governments that straddle the boundaries of municipalities,
other areas of interdependence remain problematic. A major strike between a giant corporation and a national union
can hardly be policed by a small suburban police force,
nor can such a suburb tax the property of the corporation
whose labor force swells its school enrollment when the
plant is outside its boundaries. Such fragmentation typi-

cally results in "passing the buck" of the job of integration to a higher level of government—the county or the state.

The second example above indicates the way in which the municipality itself may become an organizational actor in an intergroup situation. For, as the effective area of the economic and social city expands, the suburban municipality represents an island within the complex that may affect the city's components but is immune to the sanctions of the city polity. It may produce nuisances that violently disrupt the surrounding population's activities, and act as a barrier to the creation of facilities. This also tends to result in the movement of the task upward to another governmental level.

Finally, the municipal fragmentation of the polity, in separating the workplace and residence of many citizens into separate governmental worlds, results in an extreme form of the classic dichotomy between interests and numbers. The electors of the central city include a large proportion of the urban "have nots," but their representatives control a polity that has grave consequences for the downtown holdings of the "haves." This is accentuated by the usual party organization of the city—the central city is rapidly becoming a one-party state, and that party typically represents the working class, the Negroes, and the labor unions. Thus the powerful private governments, the corporations and their networks of economic control, are dependent upon a polity that they may not control through the electorate.

The function of the local polity as an arbiter among the basic functional groups in the city, as a maintainer and enforcer of order, and as a mechanism for the selection and execution of public enterprises, is carried out in an

extremely complex fashion as a consequence of the metropolitan fragmentation. Yet these functions are inescapable
necessities, as we have demonstrated; should the locality
group become unable to perform them, the order must be
produced at another level.

## The City: Essence and Accident

The city is a differentiated part of a relatively
large-scale society. It is the point at which the organizational roads cross; it is the key arena in which the
organizational output of one organization becomes the
input of another. At this point the control and communications center of the large-scale organizations are situated;
the city produces, processes, and transmits order to the
subsidiary parts of the society. It is large in scale, not just
because of the number of people in its borders (dense villages can spread for miles) but because of the organizational peaks from which they see and the widespread
ramifications of their actions.

Yet the city is also a spatially delimited social system.
If we define a social group by its production of a stable
order of a specific kind, the city is that inclusive locality
group that maintains the necessary order within a population constituting a major control center for large-scale society. Here dominant or subsidiary control centers for the
organizations controlling a wide range of society-wide
activities exist side by side. Within the city the integration
of activities among various functional segments of the
society takes place. Through the national market system
and the political-governmental system occur the necessary

interchanges of messages and materials for maintaining a continental society.

Other forms of order are also maintained, for the city is today the dominant form of local community. A majority of our citizens work in plants and offices clustering around the market and organizational headquarters and live in the great rings of residential settlement around the control centers. Each decade a larger proportion of all Americans live within a smaller proportion of the total space available in the nation.

Inescapable problems emerge from contiguity. These include the ordering of relations among constituent groups, maintenance of public order and safety, maintenance of the necessary plant for the physical persistence and integration of activities. These are problems inherent in the city as a spatially inclusive group. Order is maintained in part through control internal to constituent groups, through private governments within functional segments of the society, and through norms of a more inclusive group— the national social system. But key tasks remain, which can only be handled by an organization specific to the locality. This organizational level is one in which social categories of persons and "legal persons" have allocated rights and duties because of their commitment to the locality, and these rights and duties are honored by the public enforcers, the police, who represent the larger organization of those prescriptions and proscriptions. It is, in short, the urban polity.

Such a polity may be organized in many different ways, from the *podesta* system of the early Italian cities to the cumbersome machinery of the nineteenth century American city. It may integrate activities within a smaller-

scale city or a city of a smaller-scale society. This is irrelevant to the essential definition of the city as a subject of
intellectual inquiry. What is relevant and essential is the
city as a social order, a system coordinating the behavior
of many persons within a community, which in turn plays
a basic role in coordinating the behavior of its carrying
society.

# THE CITIZEN
# IN THE
# URBAN
# WORLDS

CHAPTER **3**

THE ORGANIZATIONAL transformation of the total society that is the key meaning of increasing scale whorls together the population in a few great centers of residence, work, and social activities. Migrating from Europe, Mexico, and Africa to the United States, and within the United States from the countryside to the small town, from small town to city, each decade has witnessed a progressive concentration of population in the urban areas. As this occurs, the social nature and the way of life of the average man is radically transformed.

He moves from a world in which the natural landscape and the weather are dominant into one where the landscape is largely the work of man's machines and brains, the weather largely irrelevant. He moves from an economy where the chief act was extraction of those material goods that man found valuable from mine and field and forest into an economic system given to endless refining, fabricating, elaborating, merchandising, and consuming of those materials. He moves into a system where the sweat of the brow is largely replaced by the lubrication of the machine.

He comes into the large-scale society through the urban door, bearing the marks of his origins—in his ways of dressing and speaking, his view of the nonhuman world and the social world, and the things he considers most worth achieving. As such, he is placed low on the rank order of the city dweller. (In Latin America he is identified with the despised Indio—as long as he will not change his dress and his ways.) He is the most typical "hick" the city dweller sees. But he adjusts his ways to the new world, and his children become urbanites who, in their turn, despise the newcomer. The city is a vast machine that blends the aggregate to a given constituency, then reforms it for new jobs and new ways of life.

## INDIVIDUATION AND SOCIAL DIFFERENTIATION

We have spoken of social differentiation as an attribute of a total society, defined as the variation in normative structure among subgroups. This may be translated into individuation or the probability that any two individuals will differ from each other in their controlling culture. Such individuation is due to variations in life organization and it is a consequence of the role the individual plays in the larger society. It must not be confused with "individualism"—the latter has strong value connotations and implies freedom of choice on the part of the actor as to what he will be and do. We are concerned with social differentiation and individuation because they are predictable and ineluctable consequences of changes in the scale of the society.

If we consider American society at the turn of the century as an earlier phase of increase in scale, we note three dimensions of differentiation. They are interrelated, and all are consequent to the progressive absorption of immigrants and rural persons into the networks of organization centered in cities. They are variations in occupational background, cultural background (or ethos), and rural or urban origins. Most of the new members of the society issued from agricultural village, farm, or small town, into the larger arena; they came from societies speaking different cultural languages; they came from rural localities in which kinship was a basic principle of order and children were valued as ends.

They moved into urban centers of organization, where they were amalgamated into the ongoing division of labor. This produced many bizarre and grotesque examples of cultural syncretism—for the process of amalgamation itself accentuated the variation in norms and the resulting individuation of social actors. Their original occupational skills were "crossed" with the demands of a society in which jobs were proliferating as the division of labor progressed; their lower educational achievement increased the dispersion in the direction of "no education"; the resulting division of labor and control produced an increased variation in rewards—from the entrepreneurs of expansion, the Vanderbilts, Morgans, and Goulds, to the "bohunks," "wops," and "gees" who tended the furnaces and built the railroads.

Amalgamation of populations with widely varying ethos —with family traditions, religions, and languages from the four corners of the earth—produced another wide array of social types. The acculturation continuum ranged from the conservative "orthodox" to the "bastard cultures" of their children who maneuvered for a more favorable place in the division of rewards and labor. All variants from the old American, Protestant society of the early nineteenth century were, to some degree, forced into a partial isolation and degradation of social honor: thus, being a "hyphenated" citizen was a status shared by a wide variety of persons— with its own consequences. Finally, the more intensely involved the individuals were in both the larger system and the ethnic enclave, the greater the pressure upon them to somehow reconcile their inheritance with their day-to-day necessities. From the degradation of the "hyphenated" citizen and the efforts at reconciliation of cultures emerged the "marginal man," the new cultural specimen who was neither majority nor minority, but the specific product of amalgamation. To the original differentiation resulting from the inclusion of diverse peoples in one society was added the differentiation resulting from their various efforts to relate their separate inheritances to the ongoing system.

The rural and small-town background of a large proportion of those who were integrated in the large-scale system, whether immigrant or American by birth, produced another dimension of variation. It was manifest in the variable importance of kin and family. Such variation was correlated with social class and ethnic origins, but was not identical—for some working class and ethnic individuals preserved the older order, with its central focus on home and family, while others threw off such supercargo. ("He goes farthest who goes naked and alone.") Within the densely inhabited central city where most migrants into large-scale society lived, the very organization of space militated against the older life. A generation of urban sociologists have indicated the unsuitability of the world of factory or office, tenement or apartment house, to the older family-centered social system. Others note the spatial separation of home and work, the separation of the organization of production from the organization of the family. The net result was an increasing differentiation of life style. The more wealthy, urban population had smaller families than the poor from rural localities, but some of the urban poor from rural areas adopted family limitation as children became penalties instead of rewards. Variations in life style were results both of the culture of origin and of amalgamation into the order of the urban society.

All three dimensions of differentiation were, as noted above, highly intercorrelated: the latest and most rural entrants to the system needs must take the poorly rewarded jobs, and they brought with them an ethos and a way of life that emphasized home, family, and their difference from the city folk. Such differences, in the case of the foreign-born, were stabilized and reinforced by segregation in residential subareas of the cities and were supplemented by the self-segregation of those committed to deviant and "un-American" ways of life. Segregation increased the differential association of similar populations, structuring and perpetuating the subculture. The locality area was the basis for a social form that was culturally conservative: it laid the groundwork for the "mosaic of social worlds." It was most evident in the cities, and its evidence strongly influenced the thinkers who turned urban sociology toward ecology.

Such was the general pattern of differentiation at an earlier level of societal scale. Today, the ruins of this order remain, but only as islands in the sea of a national society and culture. Amalgamation and acculturation have progressed very far, producing marked similarities throughout the system. The changes in the division of labor and rewards have tended to bring the various enclaves from small-scale society into the larger system, giving them similar positions and rewards. This has destroyed many of the barriers that segregated them in the past; the locality area is exposed to the mass media and large-scale organizational networks, and the result is acculturation to the normative structure of the larger society while the latter evolves toward a similar social definition of positions throughout the system.

At the same time, the rate of energy transformation has increased steadily for the society as a whole. While it is a necessary condition for changes in occupation and culture, its specific effect is the increased surplus available for the population's use—a surplus of wealth, leisure, and meaning (or the symbolic flow) itself. The combined effects of amalgamation, acculturation, and the increase of societal surplus have separated the dimensions of social rank, ethnicity, and life style. Their correlation steadily weakens, as there is greater variation of social rank and life style within each "ethnic" segment, greater variation in ethnicity and life style at each level of social rank, greater variation in social rank and ethnicity within each life style. The three dimensions have become, in short, three separate sets of bands across the total population of the larger society, rather than interrelated attributes of specific, locality-defined social groups.

### SOCIAL CHOICE AND THE NEW DIFFERENTIATIONS

The continuing increase in scale causes other bases of differentiation in the society to change or disappear. As ethnic or rural origins and the associated occupational backgrounds become less crucial in determining position and rewards within the system, region also becomes less important, for regional variations summarized these within an organizational autonomy characteristic of a smaller-scale society. As the nation-spanning organizational networks increase and interdependence becomes more intensive, the locality group, from neighborhood to region, loses its distinctive organizational and cultural form.

With the upward shift in the occupation of all Americans, variations in rights, duties, and subculture are less often due to scalar position (working stiff or white-collar man) and more often consequences of the specific occupational world of the job. Such distinctions as those of "situs" (the job family within which one works), modify the effects of the "collar-line."[1] More important than ever are the distinctions among various worlds of work—the worlds of Madison Avenue, the airlines, the electronics industry, or Detroit, together with the specific organizational empire within which one is a citizen. The middle executive of American Telephone and Telegraph inhabits a different milieu from his opposite number in the executive hierarchy of the Atchison, Topeka, and Santa Fe. Such vertical bases for occupational differentiation have hardly been explored as yet.

As illiteracy disappears and college graduates become a mass within the mass society, the function and consequences of educational differentiation also change radically. A society in which all citizens move (in some fashion) through twelve years of formal education, emerging with the skills that make the mass media available to them, cannot be differentiated as clearly through reference to the time spent in school. More important distinctions emerge —what kind of education (technical, commercial, or liberal arts) in what quality of educational center? And, among those who are "educationally adult" at whatever level of formal education, a major question becomes—what media are their chief "receptors" for the societal communication flow? The organizational network, the family, the mass media? Within the last, what is the relative importance of television, radio, magazines, the newspapers? Within each mass medium, what are the key organs—*Holiday* or *The Saturday Evening Post, Harper's* or *Sporting News?* The mass media, becoming more differentiated internally, provide the basis for (and result from) subcultures that cut across the national society. Such subcultures are related to formal education; it is doubtful if they can be explained by variation in the latter.[2]

As the gap in income between occupational classes that constitute the great bulk of the American labor force declines, absolute amount of income is a less dramatic differentiator. Millionaire and welfare client certainly are important categories of differentiation—but only an infinitesimal proportion of the population falls into either class. With the rise in income of blue-collar workers and the gradual disappearance of pauperism, a more important dimension emerges—variation in the central investments of income. Home, family, and children are the traditional absorbers of energy and wealth; however, with the increased freedom of choice, persons may opt for no marriage, for marriage without children, with few children, or with large families. Reciprocal to this choice is the growing number who opt for leisure—the development of "consumption as a way of life." Others still are chiefly concerned with upward mobility within one of the organizational systems—whether it is a given formally organized group or a market. Their use of surplus reflects this major investment.

The disappearance of the old, incapsulated, ethnic enclaves indicates another major change in the bases of differentiation. Acculturation proceeds rapidly, yet there are strong indications that nationality of origin lingers, beyond the third generation, as a differentiator. Ethnicity also can best be pictured, not as a configuration of attributes pertaining to a specific locality group, but rather as a "stain" across wide bands of the population. The generation of the original familial migration into large-scale society, nationality of origin, and relative segregation interact in very complex ways: in what ways are all third-generation "ethnics" alike regardless of origin? And all "Germans," regardless of generation? These are questions we can only pose at present: fixation upon census data has literally "pulled the rug" from under students of ethnicity for, aside from "nonwhites," later generations become impossible to identify by "country of birth."[3]

As noted earlier, those from non-English backgrounds may even have had a definite advantage in acculturating to large-scale society. Certainly, their own experience has contributed to a progressive "ethnicization" of that larger society. Cities have been major influences in welding a national culture, and have been disproportionately made up of foreigners; at the same time, the networks of the mass media have had more than their share of newer migrants—witness the importance of Jews, Italians, and others of ethnic identity in the movie, radio, and television industries. It does not seem too farfetched to hypothesize that much of the urbane culture of large-scale society is a product of the acculturating ethnic minorities—who have, in turn, shaped the messages of the mass media. These movers and shakers are, however, most apt to be "marginal men" with the life organization of the uncommitted, the detachment of the manipulator and the spectator. The results are that "old Americans" have been inducted into this culture shaped by recent arrivals and their children—or else have resisted these influences and perpetuated the cultural differences related to ethnic origin, but in a very different fashion from the older tacitly assumed superiority.

As life style becomes freer from the limits of occupation and ethnic origin, it becomes a more significant differentiator of the population. Newer immigrants to the metropolis may remain familistic in their way of life, simply perpetuating old ways. For the second and third generations, however, familism is a free choice. Thus, the high correlation between familism, ethnicity, and low social rank breaks down. After acculturation to the city, the urbanite rises in social rank and, perhaps, returns to a new version of the conventional family-centered existence —in the suburbs. Declining segregation by ethnic identity accompanies increasing concentration by life style; the mechanisms of the market provide alternatives to the apartment-house districts for the middle-rank populations who have chosen a family-centered mode of life. At the center of the city the highly urban districts select those who have no commitment to larger families, while suburban municipalities and small towns have concentrated in them the home-owning, family-centered populations. This segregation, in turn, produces an organizational structure and the preconditions for subcultures—which differ from many other neighborhoods within a city but manifest a high degree of similarity with neighborhoods in other cities of the large-scale society. Suburbanism as a way of life complements that "urbanism as a way of life" that is found in the center of the urban complex. Within the occupational structure of large-scale society, with its nation-wide organizational systems, within the flow of communications through the mass media, the familistic populations develop and retain new forms of the spatially defined community.[4]

## The Changing Allocation of Space in the City

Many persons have drawn ideal maps of the modern city; it has been pictured as a set of concentric circles, as circles cut by spokes into pie-shaped charts, as multiple nuclei somehow impinging upon one another and hanging together. Such models are useful as descriptive summaries for given cities at given times; however, they do not account for the changes that take place through time. A theory based upon space alone cannot account for spatial distributions that change through time.

If, however, we see space as both a barrier to inter-

action and a channel for interaction, our focus is upon
the media of extension that determine the lag in time
and the cost in energy for the integration of activities over
a given area. These costs we have summarized in the
phrase, the "space-time ratio." This ratio sets the limits
for an integrated pattern of activities and therefore provides the frame within which the composition of the city
*must* occur. This ratio does not change continuously
through time: it moves in a series of jerky transformations,
as given media become the major channels of integration,
consolidate their effects into a system, and give way in
turn to other media. Gilmore and Cottrell have spelled
out the progressive changes occurring as the city of two-
wheeled carts and foot passengers gave way to the city of
the street railway and steam railway, then the electric
street railway, and today the automobile. The congested
city of row-houses and tenements reflected the high cost
of mobility in time and energy during the nineteenth century; such areas still stand in the centers of our cities;
they represent funded energy, capital, commitments to the
technology of the past.[5]

However, our emphasis upon the expanding city, the
"exploding metropolis," should not lead us to a fixation
upon the geographical metaphor. Space itself has no given
meaning for social behavior: its meaning is always mediated
by the technologies. If we consider that meaning to lie in
the space-time ratio, we must entertain the possibility that,
in *social terms*, the contemporary metropolis may not be
spreading as rapidly as we think. The Chicago of the
horse-drawn street railway in Yerkes's day was miniature
compared with the metropolitan area of today, but when
we remember the limits of communication and accessi-

bility, it seems likely that it was just as vast to its human population. It may be that the city is, in many ways, remaining constant or even shrinking because of the effects of instantaneous communications.

As wider areas can be utilized for activities that remain just as closely coordinated as before, this has dramatic consequences for the division of labor and rewards in the city. For the division of labor, it means that the fringes of the metropolis become usable, for they are as accessible as were the locations near railroads and the downtown terminal in an earlier epoch. The motor truck and the automobile result in a displacement of function, and we see, for example, the multistoried warehouses of the downtown area give way to the horizontal warehouses of the suburban industrial "park." The changing space-time ratio for the availability of energy, as indicated in the wide accessibility of cheap electric power, has a similar result; both changes create greater locational freedom for economic enterprises.

In the division of rewards the changes make more areas accessible for residential neighborhoods. Populations that once clustered near public transportation today live in the outlying suburbs and reach their workplace as rapidly as those denizens of the congested city who formerly relied upon the streetcar. A more horizontal use of the land is possible and the row-houses and tenements, which were once the ecological fate of the factory workers, give way to the miles of tract developments far from the place of work. The decreasing cost in transportation relative to the social surplus and the decreasing time-cost relative to leisure allow the blue-collar worker a distance between home and work comparable to that which only the wealthy resident of the commuter suburb could afford in the early years of the century. Once again, however, this is dependent upon continued integration at the same level of efficiency.

Finally, as residential areas expand geographically, they are followed by those enterprises that are heavily dependent upon population concentration. The shopping centers scattered throughout suburbia are manifestations of this trend, as are certain industries more closely dependent upon work force than upon heavy transport. Declining density is accompanied by the development of subcenters of production, control, and exchange; shopping centers, branch plants, local dispatching stations (even branch offices of municipal government, as in Kansas City and Los Angeles) all indicate the displacement of certain functions from downtown. However, at the same time, centralization of control progresses, for the branch plants are still local arms of formal, extended organizations. For these reasons the subcenters tend to be highly standardized within the formal patterns of the controlling large-scale organizations.

## THE PATTERN OF PEOPLE

In the same way, the neighborhoods are standardized within the range of their residents' relations with the large-scale, carrying society. Freedom of dwelling location is set within the limits of the housing industry and the market (controlled to a degree by government): within the range of available housing, one chooses his neighborhood by his household needs and his share of the society's rewards. The results are a relative homogeneity within the neighborhoods and variation among them. Such neighborhoods provide a handy summarizing unit for a description of the pattern of people in the metropolis.

Disregarding for the moment the relationship of the neighborhoods to the rocks, rivers, and topography of the earth's surface, we turn to their social contiguity—their similarities and differences regardless of where they are distributed in the socially allocated space of the metropolitan area. Our major interest is in their variation along the dimensions of social rank, life style, and ethnicity.

The range in life style is wide indeed. In any large city there are the neighborhoods in which children are practically nonexistent, neighborhoods of apartment-house dwellers, in which single persons and childless families predominate and most of the women are members of the larger world of work, rather than the circumscribed world of the household. At the other pole are neighborhoods in which children are omnipresent and all dwelling units are detached, single-family residences. Here, the women are in constant attendance, the neighborhood flourishes, and the world of household and neighborhood sets up its own sphere in competition with those of the market, the corporation, the large-scale organizations.

However, variation in life style is not highly correlated with variation in social rank. At each level of social rank we find great variation in life style; contrariwise, each life style is found at all ranks. The neighborhoods vary independently in relation to these latter attributes, from the neighborhoods in which there are no college graduates, many persons did not go beyond the eighth grade, and nobody is an executive, to those in which the man who works with his hands is probably a servant in the household of the rich—the Main Lines, North Shores, and Westchester Counties of exurbia.

Ethnicity is another dimension. However, for most of the descendants of immigrants, the ethnic "stigmata" are disappearing. Jews originally from Germany and Russia, Catholics from Southern Europe, Lutherans from Germany and Scandinavia, are found distributed throughout the range of neighborhoods. It is true that certain ethnic groups with visible differentiation (Negroes, Puerto Ricans, Mexicans) are still highly concentrated: for them the ethnic dimension is a dichotomy; a neighborhood tends to be either all Negro or all white. And, in certain exclusive neighborhoods, many ethnic groups may be barred. With these exceptions, however, ethnicity is a dimension of neighborhoods that cuts across the other two.

Thus, the pattern of neighborhoods in the city may be imagined as a galaxy, located in an attribute space. Although it scatters tremendously in each direction, the mass of the population is in the great middle range of social rank—resident in neighborhoods of skilled craftsmen and white-collar workers with a few professionals. The galaxy leans toward the familistic end of the continuum of life styles—where homeowners tend their yards and children and women carry on a continuous flow of communication within the bounds of the neighborhood.

SUBURB AND CENTRAL CITY

Returning to an examination of geographical space, we find that few of these neighborhoods are sharply distinguished from those adjacent to them; they are physically indistinguishable acres in the endless sea of buildings.

Progression is usually gradual, from neighborhood to neighborhood, as familism increases, or social rank declines. To be sure, the dramatic extremes exist—skid row, the gold coast, exurbia, the slums—but most of the population dwells in the more prosaic worlds at the middle of the galaxy, the "lumpen middle range." They occupy the middle grounds in the worlds of work and they opt for the middle ground between familism and consumership. Their variation is further muted by the acculturation of their population to the norms of the national system through their place in the organizational network and their exposure to the mass media. Achievement is comparable at each level of life style. The tiny cracker-box bungalow of the tract development is a miniature of the sprawling ranch house of exurbia. The difference is one of degree, not one of culture.

Such differences in social geography are frequently implied in references to the suburban turn American society has taken—and the suburbs are used as prototypes to summarize the various trends of change. Suburbia however, strictly speaking, is only an artifact of the static boundary lines of the central city; most of the newer development has taken place outside these boundaries of necessity, but this does not represent a difference in kind. The same types of population live on both sides of the city limits.

The suburban areas are exaggerations, visually, of the changes in the modal life of the urban population, for they are newer commitments of energy—reflecting the increase in the surplus and the accessibility of the peripheries for the division of rewards.[6] They are horizontal and dispersed, for they are produced for the family-centered households of the middle rank, providing the *lebensraum* for the second and third generations of city dwellers who opt for familistic life styles. They may represent, in this sense, the growing edges of the culture—the trends that will dominate the entire metropolitan society of the future. For, when we concentrate upon the three population attributes that define suburbia in the ideal type (white, middle class, and familistic), we find that many neighborhoods of the central city approximate the same levels as suburbia. The central city, however, has exclusive possession of most nonassimilating ethnics (the darker-skinned migrants) and most of the very poor (the dwellers in congested, aged residential areas inherited from the earlier epoch). The suburbs have a larger and larger proportion of the very wealthy, as family styles change and the suburban child-centered ranch house supersedes the town house among the rich. But most of the suburban population falls between the two extremes as the changing space-time ratio makes the outer areas as accessible as the central city to the majority of the urban population.

The central city does have a larger concentration of those who, at every rank, choose a more urban life—those who choose single blessedness, or childless marriages, or few children. It provides, in the apartment-house districts toward the center, facilities for those whose lives are organized in reference to the job, the market, the entertainment media of the Loop or Times Square, and a scattered circle of their friends. The suburbs and the outer neighborhoods of the central city are, conversely, more suitable to the child-rearing family. This division of rewards in the form of residence is, at the same time, related to the life cycle. Those who have not yet married, not yet had children, find the central city an adequate site for their activities, but with the commitments to a family, the suburbs become a logical residence. The relative values of time and convenience shift with the commitments implied in life style, and these frequently shift as the individual goes through the family cycle.

Thus, the "ideal type" approach to central city-suburban differences is less than adequate. It represent a dichotomy supported only at the level of local government. For the most part, the two halves of the metropolis represent different configurations of the same attributes, different "mixes" of the same population types. They are at the same time indissolubly tied together in a common local labor force, within the bounds of a common local economy. The expressway interchange in the center of the city makes possible their scattered residences and common work places.

# Individual Participation
# in Metropolitan Society

Such are, in crude terms, the social types that make up the vast majority of the metropolitan citizenry. They constitute the roots of the urban polity, for they are the voters who act on issues and personnel of the urban area's government; they are the taxpayers whose incomes furnish the resources of polity; they are also, in their demands for service and their violation of the norms, the "problems" of the urban polity. With the great weight given to sheer numbers in our society, the average citizen multiplied by the thousandfold is the key actor in the polity of the urban community.

In the past the hierarchical and usually hereditary orders of a small-scale society divided the job of control. Compliance was assured through a traditional normative structure. We have seen how the large-scale metropolitan community dissolves these traditional orders, going far beyond the destruction of hereditary ruling classes to blur and weaken the distinctive prerogatives associated with race, nativity, and social class itself. This weakening of differential rights and duties has two faces. For some it is "equality," for others, "the state of the masses."

The general ideology identifying the problem and indicating its solution is, for most Americans, some variation of the democratic dogma. For the hierarchical order of the past is substituted an order based upon individual option and control through the consent of the governed. In making such normative decisions, however, one is also making certain assumptions about the empirical nature of modern society. One of these is the existence, at some level, of subcommunities in which the individual has interest, influence, and concerning which he has some realistic information. Such subcommunities are the necessary condition for individual participation in the vast totality of society (though they are not sufficient conditions) and whoever says "democracy" is, in effect, positing them.

Such groups have been, in the main, defined by geographical space. The political community in modern society, with few exceptions, has been defined as the population living within given territorial bounds. Whether in electing a president or a dogcatcher, the unit has been precinct, ward, township, city, county, or province. Thus, the larger society is brought close to home, and the citizen votes among friends and neighbors. His representation at the seats of power is, in turn, a result of his residence in the spatially defined political unit.

However, the continuous increase in scale of America since its democratic birth has worked radical changes in the nature of locality groups. This centralized and city-centered society differs radically from the nation postulated by the framers of the democratic constitutions. And, while the rural population and the smaller cities still have their importance, the social structure of the metropolis is crucial for the study of social participation and the political process in contemporary America.

Many of the current images of the city sharply contradict the empirical assumptions implied in the democratic dogma. Those who emphasize the dissolution of the community and the growth of mass society, Spengler, Ortega, Durkheim, Tonnies, and others, forecast an increasingly complex and heterogeneous society in which order results from the functional interdependence of organized groups and solidarity within groups leads to dynamic relations among them.[7] As a corollary, the most powerful organized group, the state, grows in relative importance. Such views are congruent with the analyses of Georg Simmel and Louis Wirth, who emphasize these social aspects of the city: (a) its heterogeneity, (b its impersonality, (c) its anonymity, (d) the consequent social fragmentation of the individuals who make up the urban world.[8] In this view (there are important differences among these theorists, but in major respects they are similar) the primary group structure of society is in a process of rapid dissolution, and, with it, the primary community. Kinship groups, neighborhood groups, the church, and the locality group are losing their importance. Their strength in controlling individual behavior has shifted to formal, secondary groups, that organize work, religion and politics. Even play is controlled by the large commercial organizations.

From such a position, the theorist who wishes to emphasize the viability of democratic structures must, like MacIver, accept the formal organization as the effective subcommunity—one that is capable of performing the function of organizing individuals in meaningful wholes that may then participate in the larger society. The "Associational Society" is seen as the alternative to the hierarchical society based upon a locality group.[9] The exclusive organizations that are relatively free of any given locale can better represent (for they involve more deeply) the citizen of the larger society than can a "local community" having little real meaning.

These formulations concerning urban social structure are largely the result of keen observation and analysis, rather than reliable empirical studies. Their influence is due to two facts: they are based upon observations available at random in the center of any large city, and they fill, neatly, a gap in the theoretical system of sociology. However, in recent years a substantial body of work has been accumulated dealing with the specific area of participation in the urban community. It is possible, with this work in mind, to sketch a tentative description of the modes of participation occurring among urbanites—a snapshot of the organizational topography of the metropolitan area. Such a description serves as a test of the earlier assumptions and the basis for new inferences.

# The Disenchantment of the City: Empirical Research

The people of the city have come from the four corners of the earth; their grandfathers were country boys in the city, peasants from the Ukraine, or dirt farmers from the backwoods of New York, Iowa, Oregon, or Alabama. Only a few generations ago most of their forebears were illiterate or barely able to read and write. They have moved into a world where the rewards for effort are greater than their ancestors ever dreamed possible, but a world where they are also forced to accept a great deal of freedom. In contrast to the society of village or small town, few of the people whom they know care where they spend their money and time, and they have more of both than the necessities of life require. We shall try to plot out some of the ways in which they spend their time.

The studies to be summarized are focused upon participation in formal organizations (Komarovsky), the local area as community (Janowitz), the urban neighborhood (Foley and Fava) and these together with other areas of participation (Axelrod, Bell, Greer). The urban complexes included are New York (Komarovsky and Fava), Chicago (Janowitz), Los Angeles and St. Louis (Greer), San Francisco (Bell), Detroit (Axelrod) and Rochester (Foley).[10] The net is thus spread wide, and the results are remarkably consistent—so much so that this discussion will emphasize common trends rather than variations. The following kinds of participation will be discussed: kinship, the neighborhood, the local area, formal organizations, friends, work associates, and the mass media.

*Kinship.* One of the most striking results of this research is the extreme importance of kin relations to urban residents. Sociologists, convinced that large-scale, urban society depends less and less upon the network of kinship, have de-emphasized the family as a powerful integrative structure. Yet the conjugal family is of basic importance; the urbanite, in any local area, is apt to spend most of his evenings in the bosom of his family. This is true even in Hollywood, and extremely so in the suburbs. Furthermore, even the extended family is important; one-third of the Los Angeles sample visited uncles, cousins, and the like at least monthly. These relationships were more than casual gossiping; studies in Detroit indicate that mutual aid among members of an extended family is a very important resource for the individual household.

*The Neighborhood.* There is much more differentiation here—the range is from local areas in which a substantial number of people are intense neighbors to those in which most people hardly know any of their neighbors. The average urban resident has some informal neighboring relationships, but they are not one of the mainstays of his life. He values highly the neighbor who is a "nice person and leaves you alone."

*The Local Residential Area.* Much like their behavior as neighbors, the "local community" identification and participation of urban residents varies widely. Janowitz found that a majority of his Chicago samples identified their local area as their true home, and the same was true in Los Angeles and St. Louis. When, however, people were asked (in these latter cities) if there was another part of the metropolitan region in which they would rather live, the proportion who agreed varied from nearly zero to over half.

*Formal Organizations.* Although a majority of urban residents belong to churches, a minority, which varies around 40 per cent, attend as frequently as once a month. Aside from their church participation, most urban individuals belong to one organization or none. Individuals of low and middle social rank usually belong to one other organization at most; it is usually work-connected for men, child- or church-connected for women. Only in the upper socioeconomic levels is the "joiner" to be found with great frequency. When attendance at organizations is studied, some 20 per cent of the memberships are usually "paper memberships."

*Friendship.* Informal participation in friendship relations, with individual friends or friendship circles, is an extremely frequent occurrence. Friendship, outside any organizational context, is a near universal in the city. The urbanite is seldom completely isolated from this type of primary relationship.

*Work Associates as Friends.* Here one of the important hypotheses of urban theory is in question. As the primary community and neighborhood decline, friendship was expected to be more closely related to work organization. However, these studies indicate that, regardless of neighboring or community participation, work associates are a minor proportion of the individual's primary relations when he is away from the job. Only in the upper socioeconomic levels (where friendship is frequently instrumental for economic ends) or unmarried working women (where work substitutes for kinship as a predictable social setting) is there a change. For the most part, work relations are insulated from the free, primary group participation of the urban dweller.

*Mass Entertainment.* Cultural participation in organized entertainment is relatively unimportant for urban adults. Most of the Los Angeles samples attended fewer than three events a month; one-third attended no event, one-third one or two, and a few attended as many as ten or more. Most of their attendance was at movies, but the real importance of the mass entertainment media was in the home. Television and radio are extremely important, but in the context of family participation.

The urbanite's individual path through social structure crosses these six areas of possible involvement and participation. According to one theory of urban society, his involvement should be increasingly intense with respect to formal organizations, work associates as friends, and mass entertainment, as we move toward the extremely urbane neighborhoods. And in these neighborhoods of apartment houses and small households, we should find a correspondingly weak relationship with kinfolk, neighbors, the local community, and primary groups other than these.

Instead, the usual individual's involvement in formal organizations and work-based friendship is weak in any type of neighborhood. The mass media are most important in a family context. Participation with kin and friendship circles is powerful, but with neighbors and the local community's groups it varies immensely by area. Although highly urbanized populations are not typical of most city dwellers (they are an extreme of a continuum) those who do exist deviate widely from the stereotype of the atomistic man. They are greatly involved in the family and kinship group, and they participate intensively in friendships and cliques. Nor do they manifest anomie, that despair Durkheim postulated as resulting from the lack of social norms and group controls. They live their lives in relative isolation from neighborhood, community, and voluntary organization, but they compensate by intensive involvement in primary relationships with kinfolk and friends.

However, the majority of the population in a great urban complex does not lie in the highly urbanized segments; instead, it is of middle to low urbanism and middle social rank. And, the less urban the neighborhood, the greater the involvement of its residents in voluntary organizations and the greater their concern for, and participation in, neighborhood and local community. The local area becomes a social fact, as well as a geographical site for activity.

The picture that emerges is of a society in which the conjugal family is extremely powerful among all types of population. This small, primary group structure is one basic area of involvement; at the other pole is work, a massive absorber of time, but an activity that is rarely related to the family through "outside" friendship with on-the-job associates. Instead, the family, its kin, and its friendship group, is relatively free-floating, within the world of large-scale secondary associations. Burgess has pointed out that the weakening of a primary community results in the increasing relative dependence of individuals upon the conjugal family as a source of primary relationships; this same principle explains the persisting importance of extended kin and the proliferation of close friendships in urban America.[11] In the metropolis the community as a solid phalanx of friends or acquaintances does not exist; if individuals are to have a community in the older sense of *communion*, they must make it for themselves. These conditions are at an extreme in the highly urban neighborhoods, and there friendship and kinship are, relatively, most important in the average individual's social world. In other kinds of neighborhoods the family is usually identified, although weakly, with the local community; it "neighbors," but strictly within bounds. By and large, the conjugal family group keeps itself to itself; outside is the world—formal organizations, work, and the communities.

Such a picture is remarkably similar to that which Oeser and Hammond present, from their studies of Melbourne, Australia.[12] Melbourne, like the American cities studied, is a mushrooming metropolitan complex in a large-scale and highly urbanized society. Its people are mostly of middle social rank, neither poor nor wealthy. Its social order centers around the single-family dwelling unit, the conjugal family, selected kinfolk, the job, and the mass media—the latter consumed in the home. Like urban Americans, the residents of Melbourne are avid fans of the various spectator sports and "do-it-yourself" activities. Neither in Melbourne nor in American cities do we find much participation, by most people, in formal organizations or the community. The society of Australia is, if anything, less hierarchical than that of America (many of its citizens have no desire to recall their family lineage). Control is by universal ballot and all must, by law, participate in elections. Yet the family retires to its domain, as in the American cities studied, to work in the garden, listen to radio or television, care for children and read the products of the mass media.

Such findings as these are important in two respects: first, in their sharp departures from an older, conventional picture of metropolitan life, and secondly, in their cor sistency. The agreement among the various Americ studies, and between these and the Australian study, lead us to suspect that such participation patterns are a result of the powerful trends associated with increasing scale in modern Western society.

The increasing surplus and changing space-time ratio of large-scale society, and its consequent freedom from older constraints, has allowed a wide range of choice for the individual household. This is manifest in the great variation in life styles that a contemporary metropolitan population exhibits. It ranges from the family-centered, home-centered life at the familistic pole to an opposite pole of extreme urbanism, where one finds many single individuals and couples without children. The utility of different parts of the metropolis for different styles of life results in a concentration of similar persons with similar needs in given neighborhoods.

Thus, the galaxy of local residential areas making up a metropolis exhibit, at each level of social rank, vast differences between the highly urban neighborhoods and the familistic neighborhoods. In general, the highly urban neighborhoods lie within the central city and the familistic areas lie in the outer rings of the central city and in the suburbs. One may keep in mind the image of the urban apartment-house districts, on one hand, and the tract developments on the other. The important thing is not, however, location in geographical space, but *life style*. Typically "urban" neighborhoods occur in the suburban municipalities, "suburban" neighborhoods in the central city.

As one moves across the continuum, from the urban toward the familistic neighborhoods, community participation in the local area increases. Studies in Los Angeles, Chicago, and St. Louis, have indicated that the urbanism of an area is closely associated with the importance of the locality group—geographical space becomes social fact.

The results of the Los Angeles study of four census-tract populations at middle social rank, without segregated populations but varying from very urbane to very familistic, were summarized as follows.

> In general, our findings indicate a growing importance of the local area as a social fact, as we go from the highly urbanized areas . . . to the low-urban areas. Neighboring, organizational location in the area, the residences of the members of organizations in the area, the location and composition of church congregations, all vary with urbanism and increase as urbanism decreases. Readership of the local community press also increases, as does the ability to name local leaders and intention to remain in the area indefinitely.

> Thus the studies of the small community, with its local organizational structure and stratification system, may apply in the low-urban areas: they are not likely to fit in the highly urban area. We may think of the urbanism dimension as having, at the low-urban pole, communities much like those studied by W. Lloyd Warner, August Hollingshead, and others. At the highly urbanized pole, we encounter the big city population of the stereotype, organized not in community terms, but in terms of the

corporation, politics, the mass media and the popular culture. But predominantly, the highly urban populations associate in small, informal groups, with friends and kinfolk.[13]

Further studies, which included interviews with a cross section of the entire population of metropolitan St. Louis, Missouri, support these findings. These data are reinforced by the conclusions of Janowitz, who found, among his Chicago sample, that "Family cohesion and primary group contacts seemed more relevant for predisposing an individual toward acceptance of the community's controlling institutions and associations."

Thus, few urban subareas approach the anonymity and fragmentation of the stereotype. However, fewer still approach the kind of subcommunity envisaged in the democratic ideology. Although more respondents can name local leaders in the suburbs than in the highly urbanized areas (in both Los Angeles and St. Louis) only some 40 per cent can do so anywhere. And a majority cannot name even one metropolitan leader. With this qualification in mind, the differences between the polar extremes are sharp and suggestive. The great variation in life style existing in the contemporary metropolis is accompanied by great variation in the social structure of its locality groups.

## Implications for the Democratic Dogma

The results of this brief summary may now be compared with the empirical assumptions underlying democratic political structures. Much of that ideal pattern relies upon the belief in stable subcommunities, viable wholes through which the individual may clarify in social discourse and affect through social action the objects of his desires and grievances. Such a locality group requires sufficient communication and involvement to result in the ordering of individual behavior. It must then be important to a large part of its constituency. Our ideal example from the past is the New England township, and its image still has an overpowering importance in our thinking. It is something of a political and social archetype.

The local area today however, particularly in the metropolis, does not represent such a community. Instead, it is necessarily what Janowitz calls a "community of limited liability." The individual's investment is relatively small in the interactional network that constitutes the locality group, and if his losses are too great he can cut them by getting out—the community cannot hold him. Even among the most community-oriented, "small-town-like" areas within the metropolis, there is great variation in the importance of the local area to the individual. The local merchants have more of a stake than the home-owning residents with children, and these have more invested than the couple without children who rent an apartment (though the latter are very rare in such neighborhoods). However, even the most deeply involved can withdraw from the local community and satisfy all needs elsewhere—and the withdrawal need not be physical.

The older definition of community posited a spatially defined social aggregate that is a powerful social group. Such groups exist only when there is functional interdependence (as the local community in the suburbs is most necessary to its merchants, least so to the childless couple who rent their dwelling). Interdependence, in turn, means commitment to the ongoing social system. Such interdependence and commitment produce intensive participation and the development of common values and norms. Constraint, in this sense, is the key to community.

If this is true, then the great degree of freedom for individual location and action in large-scale society makes the "primary community" impossible. Exceptions occur only in a few survivals, such as the Appalachian backwoods, or institutional aggregates such as the prison, monastery, and army. Aside from these atypical collectives, however, there *are* groups in which the individual must interact continuously and for a large share of his waking life. Most important is the work organization.

The functional interdependence, the flow of communication, and the consequent ordering of behavior in the place of work bulk large in the individual's life. Some theorists, of whom Mayo is the best known, imply that a primary community of work is therefore possible.[14] Certainly, economic production, a share in the surplus, and status in the general society are basic functional supports of such primary communities as the peasant village. In our society they are typically provided through membership in large-scale, extended, formal organizations. However, in a most cursory inspection of the organization of modern industry, several factors appear that make such a strong work community very unlikely. These include freedom of labor, the divorce of work and household, the conflicting functions of the work organization, and their results in the labor union on one hand and the hierarchical organization of industry on the other.[15]

Free labor, which is functional for the total economic

system, allows the individual to leave a given work group
and join another at will. His needs may be served as
well or better—and likewise the functional demands of
industry. This freedom is reinforced by the complete
divorce between his household group and work group;
the job is left at the factory or office, and can be changed
or discarded like a suit of social clothes. However, his
relations with others in the work group are conditioned
by this freedom. Even work is a commitment of limited
liability.

Equally important is the hierarchical organization of
work in our society. The "scalar principle" is undoubtedly
necessary in large organized groups; still the net effect is
that the most time-absorbing social group outside the
family is ordered in a way contradictory to the assumptions of democratic process. Further, the common interest of workers and management is so channeled, through
the unstable division of the social product into profits
and wages, as to create a well-structured division of interest as well. This schism between the leaders of work
and their followers drastically reduces the common ground
of values and the effective norms. The unions have risen
as a response.

Finally, the division of labor is so great as to weaken
the common conscience of the different levels of workmen. Durkheim postulated a solidarity, a group *élan*, based
upon teamwork. However, to the routine worker his job
is frequently merely the payment of a pound of flesh.
A large proportion of the membership of most work
organizations is made up of routine workers, and their
lack of control over their work, their competition with
management for economic rewards, their organized voice,

the union, and their ability to leave the job, all represent limiting conditions. It is difficult to see how strong communities could arise within such market-oriented organizations.

Thus, the major organizational segment of society that orders work is unable to supply the basis for primary community. The local area is functionally weak. The kinship system is important, but in a "privatized" manner. The remaining possible structure for individual participation is the formal voluntary organization. A brief review of the findings cited earlier, however, indicates that such organizations are relatively unimportant at the grass roots. They are arenas for intensive participation to only a small minority of their members; many urban individuals have no formal organizational membership at all.

One possible exception is the labor union. Here is an organization whose functional importance for its members is great indeed. Unlike industry it is an organization based upon the assumptions of the democratic ideology; participation in decision-making is quite easy. Finally, it is a type of organization that is extremely widespread—it is probably the most important single kind of formal organization outside the churches, as measured by size of membership. Many have noted these facts and have interpreted the union as the worker's true community. What of union participation?

Many studies indicate that the average attendance of members at a local union's routine meetings is extremely low—from less than 1 per cent to perhaps 20 per cent. Most of those who attend are the same group, over and over, and these together with the paid professional staff have undue influence upon the organizational decisions.

For the average member, on the other hand, the union is almost an aspect of government. He pays his dues and, as in the national elections, frequently does not vote. His leaders, with the best will in the world, far overreach their responsibility—for there is nobody else to take responsibility. Most often the leaders "run the locals" with some restraint from the small cadre of actives and the members are, in Herberg's phrase, "a plebiscitary body."[16] Far from constituting a real community for the workers, the union is largely another service organization. It can mobilize the members to strike, but not to participate in the routine functioning where the basic grounds for strikes are considered and argued out.[17]

## An Embarrassment of Freedom

It is apparent that, in a society with a democratic political structure and ideology, democratic social processes are relatively rare. Shared decision-making, control through consent, is probably most common in the kinship and friendship groups, but it is hardly transmitted through them to larger entities. The other areas where individual participation is possible, the local community and the formal organization, engage only a minority in more than token participation, and the organizations of work —most important of all in many respects—are structurally unfit for democratic processes as work is organized in our society. The following picture of participation in metropolitan society results.

There are a plethora of formal organizations, labor unions, business and professional groups, churches and church-related groups, parent-teacher associations, and the like. They exert pressure and they influence the political party—another formal organization. However, the leadership in such organizations is largely professionalized and bureaucratized, and such leaders become, in effect, oligarchs. At the same time the members participate in an extremely erratic manner, and frequently "stay away in droves" from the meetings. The organization is a holding company for the members' interests; they exercise an occasional veto right in the plebiscites.

The local area is not a community in any sense, in the highly urban parts of the city; it is a community "of limited liability" in the suburbs. Communication and participation are as apt to be segmental as in any formal organization that is extraterritorial. And many are utterly uninvolved, even in the strongest spatially defined communities.

Formal government is highly bureaucratized and, aside from votes in national elections and (occasionally) in local elections, the individual participates very little. Most party clubs are made up of professionals, semiprofessionals, a handful of actives, and a large majority of paper members.

The organization of work is nondemocratic in its control structure and the individual's participation is largely a matter of conforming to directions and implementing decisions made far above him in the hierarchy. This is of basic importance, for, with the rise of professional leadership in all formal organizations—from labor unions to Boy Scouts, the most intense participation in all groups is apt to be that of the official, for whom the organization is his *job* in a job hierarchy.

Thus, interpreting the participation of the average individual in the polity of metropolitan society is a somewhat bizarre experience. By and large he does not participate. Since this is true, it is difficult to make a case for the widespread importance of the democratic processes in the everyday behavior of most people except in the home and friendship circle. The democracy we inhabit is, instead, largely a democracy of substantive freedoms, or freedom from restraint. Produced by struggles among various professionally directed interest groups, largely quite undemocratic in their control processes, freedom of choice for the individual is something of a by-product. It exists through the balance of countervailing forces, in work, at the market place, and in government.

This freedom is, however, a considerable area of the average person's life space. It is manifest in the metropolitan resident's ability to choose marriage or single status, children or not, large family or small. It is also apparent in his freedom to choose his local residential area, and his degree of participation in its social structure—his life style. He may privatize his nonworking world and turn inward to his single-family dwelling unit and his conjugal family (which he does); he may refuse to participate in many public activities and yield only a token participation in others (and he does).

Though his commitments to the job and the family are constant and have a priority in time and energy, he exercises freedom of choice—in the market, the large sphere which Riesman calls consumership.[18] He also has a freedom in the symbol spheres that has never been widespread before in any society—the variety of media and of messages are overwhelming. There are some one thousand hours of television available each week to the Los Angeles resident. His relative wealth, literacy, and privacy allow an exploration of meaning never possible before to the rank and file of any society. In his home life he experiments with leisure. The hobby industries, the do-it-yourself industries, the flood of specialized publications and programs, bear testimony to the increasing use the urbanite makes of this opportunity. He is part of the *nouveaux riches* of leisure.

His wealth is a result of the increasing social surplus, produced by advancing technologies of energy transformation and social organization. It is a surplus of material products, of time, and of symbols. His rise is also a measure of the leveling of the hierarchical orders. Their remnants persist, in the relatively higher rates of competence, participation and leadership for the upper social ranks in most of the formal organizations. Most people, however, are the descendants, and in some respects, equivalents, of the illiterates of a hundred years ago. They have neither the vested interest in, nor the tradition of responsible participation in the life of the polity. And they have great freedom from forced participation in work. They exercise it in fashioning the typical life patterns adumbrated, in avoiding organizations, politely giving lip service to the neighbors and local community leaders, avoiding work associates off the job, orienting themselves toward evenings, week ends, and vacations. These they spend *en famille*, traveling, looking at television, gossiping and eating with friends and kin, and cultivating the garden.

The bureaucratic leadership and the plebiscitary membership, the community of limited liability and the privatized citizen, are not images most Americans hold of a proper democratic society. On the other hand, the picture is less frightening than that of the atomistic man adrift in mass society, anomic and destructive. Furthermore, the ideal picture of participation in the primary political community is a strenuous one. Perhaps a revision downward, toward effective communities of limited liability and effective plebiscites might be more congruent with the organizational structure of large-scale society.

# THE

# COMMUNITY

# OF

# LIMITED

# LIABILITY

CHAPTER **4**

ACH GENERATION of Americans is more mobile than its fathers were. The wide face of the continent has become a single system, and each year households within its bounds move from country to city, from city to city, and from neighborhood to neighborhood within the metropolitan complex.[1] (Los Angeles, an extreme case, reported in 1950 that 24 per cent of its population lived in another residence a year earlier.[2]) We have been called a "nation of nomads," but our movement is necessary for the flexible deployment of human resources in a large-scale and expanding society. It is a sign, a measure of social metabolism indicating the change and expansion of the larger system.

This mobility leads some to speak of "rootlessness." Mobility does indicate our dependence upon larger exclusive membership organizations, weakening the constraint of the local community upon its members. The weaker commitment to local area as a home, the lack of a lifetime investment in neighborhood and community, and the overriding importance of occupation have led some to speak disparagingly of metropolitan neighborhoods as "dormitories" and "bedroom communities."[3]

The contingent commitment of Americans to their local area has resulted in two drastic transformations of the locality as a social structure. First, land in America is typically seen as transferable *property*, rather than *place*. The ancestral home and hallowed ground are anomalies in a society were residential change is so widespread and frequent. The process of increase in scale has so altered the use of land and the shape of the community, from farm neighborhood to central city, as to diminish the unique social values of given places. Second, the displacement of many important activities from the locality of residence has weakened the interactional network of the local area. As common tasks disappear, so does social interaction as a value in its own right. And such interaction is one major basis for that flow of communication which generates a normative structure and a primary dimension. Thus the communion of those who share a locality is weakened, and the primary community fades away.[4]

But the local residential community still encompasses some very crucial structures, and therefore has a constraining force upon its members. This is particularly true of those who have chosen a familistic life in the areas of low urbanism. They have made major commitments of income and time. The house they own absorbs a constant amount of income. The children they beget require a growing investment of money; at the same time they eliminate the possibility of a second income through the wife's working. Furthermore, while the life style is chosen because our society can afford a large degree of freedom in everyday life, the choice is still subject to limitations. The financing of the familistic households includes a major investment of time—in the maintenance of the home, in the business of child-rearing, in all the ways one can substitute hours for dollars. This investment of time increases steadily as the supply of leisure increases. Though the suburban neighborhood is not the site of the husband's occupation, he spends most of his free time there—sixty or seventy hours each week. And, for his wife and children, the residential neighborhood is the center of the world. The bedroom community is, in many matters, the basic community.

## The Functional Basis of the Local Community in the Metropolis

We have noted earlier that the lifeways of urban populations have become differentiated on a continuum ranging from a familistic to an extremely urban mode of life. Such a continuum first emerged from the analysis of census-tract populations—relatively homogeneous residential areas defined by the Bureau of the Census for the study of subareas in the metropolis. Thus the indexes developed to measure life style apply to such aggregates. At the high urbanism pole we find neighborhoods where single persons, childless couples, and one-child families predominate. At the opposite end we find the single-family dwelling units inhabited by families with several children, where the woman's role is that of wife and mother instead of a participant in the labor force.

The familistic type of neighborhood approximates, of course, the typical stereotype of suburbia. Although suburbs have no monopoly on such populations, we have seen that they are more consistently inhabited by familistic populations than any other part of the metropolis. In the suburbs the new housing developments make available, at relatively modest costs, the sites that allow for the play of children in safe and "pleasant" places, space for growing and harvesting grass, flowers, and vegetables, for keeping pets, for patio exercise, and the like. Suburban residents who have been asked to compare their home with the central city have emphasized the physical and social facilities for child-raising—and high on the rank order is private space, inside and out. The changing space-time ratio has provided such living sites in abundance on the peripheries, and the vast middle range of metropolitan society has taken advantage of the resources.[5]

The local associational structure of a population is closely related to such characteristics as the familism of a neighborhood. Contiguity indicates the likelihood of contact, homogeneity the likelihood of similar interests, and life style itself the specific content of those interests. And, in the main, the less urban and more familistic the neighborhood, the more important is the dwelling unit as a site for everyday life, and for a particular kind of life.

To repeat, however, geographical contiguity has no self-evident social meaning. It may become the basis for interdependence only when it constitutes a field for social action. There are three fields, concentric in scope, that constitute the social structure of "the community of limited liability." These are the neighborhood, the local residential enclave (or local area), and (in the suburbs) the municipality. Each is the basis for a group, for each is "an aggregate in a state of functional interdependence, from which emerges a flow of communication and a consequent ordering of behavior."[6]

### THE NEIGHBORHOOD

When the residents of a neighborhood are households with familistic ways of life there is a high probability of intersecting trajectories of action. Surrounding households are important and inescapable parts of any given household's environment, and there emerge problems of social order, maintenance, and mutual aid. It is necessary to regulate the play of children, child-adult relations, and adult relations, to the degree that these are inevitable, for misunderstanding or conflict may represent blocks to the orderly performance of the household's way of life. When sites overlap visually, aurally, and sometimes physically, it is necessary to regulate the use of the scene: the unsightly yard, the noisy night air, and the dangerously barricaded sidewalk constitute such blocks. And the very similarity of life routines produces similar equipment and tasks, making the interchangeability of parts a possibility.

Mutual aid ranges from the traditional borrowing of a cup of bourbon to the baby-sitting pool.

Certainly, interdependence exists in the apartment-house districts (though to a smaller degree), but the structure of the neighborhood and life style of the population bring about a different kind of order. The low rate of communication, due to the lack of common or overlapping space and separation of life routines in time, results in a greater dependence upon rules of the building, laws of residency, and formal authorities to enforce them. The lesser commitment that results from renting makes it a simple matter, when order breaks down, to cut one's losses and leave. In the highly urban neighborhood the apartment-house manager and police are important enforcers; the utility of such an organization of space, from household to *concierge* to police, is evident in the reliance placed upon it by the state in Europe. In the familistic neighborhoods, however, life style and the relationships among the sites forces interhousehold communication and allows neighborhood organization.

Communication in the neighborhood may take place at many levels, but viewing it as an organizational unit the most important level is in casual interaction among those whose paths must cross. In adjoining backyards, at bus stop, school and corner grocery, on sidewalks and playgrounds, interaction is unavoidable with "the neighbors." It may become elaborated into relatively personal relationships—friendship and clique—but these must be distinguished from the neighborhood as an organization, just as we distinguish friendship within any enterprise from the ongoing structure of activity common to the group.

The resulting patterns of behavior probably vary a good deal by neighborhood. However, the ubiquity of the phrase "the good neighbor" indicates a generalized role system and normative structure. Friendliness, orderliness, accessibility in time of need, cleanliness, are important characteristics of a commonly conceived role. They are, however, rooted in the interdependence of a neighborhood.[7] Individuals conform to such norms (whether they love their neighbor or not) because the norms facilitate their ongoing household enterprises, and in their conforming they in turn bring pressure to bear upon their neighbors.

The neighborhood, however, is a microcosm. It is a precipitate of interacting households, but participation in a neighborhood does not necessarily indicate a role in the larger local area as community or political unit. It produces, at the least, some order among the small enclave of residents, some communication relevant to the nearby scene.

### THE LOCAL RESIDENTIAL AREA

Neighbors in familistic areas have similar interests, for their life styles have the same prerequisites. Interdependence among those living in the larger residential area results when similar interests are transformed into common interests, based on the common field in which they must act. Public schools and governmental services are usually available only through residence in a spatially defined aggregate; commercial goods and services are distributed throughout a given spatial radius. To the degree that vital resources for the households are involved, the population of a local residential area is functionally interdependent. At the same time space as the common site of everyday activities (the street, the sidewalk, the park, and the playground) is a basis of interdependence, as in the neighborhood.

The local residential community includes a number of neighborhoods. It may or may not be coterminous with a political unit; leaving this question aside for the moment, let us consider the organizational structure of such local areas. The grounds for interdependence have been sketched in; communication relevant to the area ordinarily takes place through two channels—the community press and the voluntary organizations in the locale. While each is a channel for local news, the organizations are more important in ordering behavior while the press is mostly a communications channel.

The local community press is widely distributed and widely read; it is a medium available to almost all residents of most local areas. Its utility stems directly from the interdependence of activities within the local area; supported by local merchants, it provides support in turn for the various formal organizations constituting the community as an interactional system. To be sure, all areas are not serviced by a community press today, but, so useful is the medium (and consequently, so lucrative) it is rapidly covering the residential areas of the metropolis. It develops where there is a rich market for its services, however, and this occurs most consistently among the familistic populations—where it is read most widely and carefully.[8]

The local community press in the metropolis has been described by Janowitz. It is parochial in its interests, reporting almost exclusively upon local happenings, translating metropolitan events into their effects upon the local scene, and seldom reporting national events. Local personages—merchants, bureaucrats, organizational leaders, and others, are the actors on this stage. Insofar as the area is a social fact it is reflected in the press and reinforced in the process. In perpetuating lines of communication, the paper stabilizes norms and roles. If it is chiefly a merchandising mechanism in its economic function (as is true of the metropolitan dailies) it is also a public platform and bulletin board for the area in its social and political functions.

Turning now to the ordering of behavior, when we consider a local area that has no separate government, we must emphasize the order resulting from participation in (and response to) the voluntary formal organizations sited there. Such organizations are segmental in membership and purpose, including only those who are dependent upon them for basic needs of their household and who volunteer for duty. Community-oriented associations, improvement associations, child-centered organizations, fraternal and service clubs, are particular to the area; their membership is largely limited to those living there, and they are instruments of persuasion and control with respect to various community problems, projects, and festivals. If there is no political structure they are the only existing groups through which an interdependence specific to the area (issuing in local problems) communicated through the press (as community issues) can become manifest in social action.

There is, however, a political unit roughly coterminous with the spatially based social system in many familistic areas lying outside the boundaries of the central city.

## THE SUBURBAN MUNICIPALITY

The typical political structure of metropolitan suburbia seen as a whole is a crazy quilt of many small municipalities having various eccentric shapes and displaying little obvious order in their boundaries. However, many of these municipalities are roughly coterminous with one or more social communities of the sort discussed above. When this is true, the seemingly arbitrary lines on the map come to represent a social fact. The common field of activity (and the various segmental interests organized by this field) are contained within a structure having the power to control, within wide limits, some of the basic goods and services of the residents. The layout and maintenance of streets, parks, schools, the shape of commercial and residential developments, are not only sources of interdependence for those committed to the place—their control is so managed that effective action by the interdependent population is possible. Beyond this, taxation, the police power, the right to license and control, are assigned to the municipality as they cannot be to a local area in the absence of specific formal government. In this sense the municipality creates further bases for interdependence and a more powerful local community.

## RELATIONS AMONG ORGANIZATIONAL LEVELS

The organizational structure of the populations in the metropolis may be summarized as follows:

1. Overlapping activities of households result in neighborhoods, which exist as a kind of single thread network throughout the familistic population. (Neighborhoods overlap as do households, and the neighborhood structure

of a metropolis resembles St. Augustine's definition of God, an infinite circle whose center is everywhere and whose periphery nowhere.)

2. Larger residential areas with a degree of interdependence constitute "communities of limited liability." They exhibit a flow of communication through the community press and informal interaction, and order behavior through voluntary organizations.

3. In the suburbs, political units are frequently coterminous with one or more social communities. In these cases, there is a political community.

The four types of organization dealt with (household, neighborhood, residential area, and municipality) are, generally, of ascending order as to size and descending order as to the probability of face-to-face, or "primary," relations. They are arranged in an order that indicates an increasing likelihood of common public interest and action, and therefore, policy formation. Thus, as a polity becomes possible, representation rather than universal participation is a necessity.

The neighborhood is very likely to generate interhousehold friendships and visiting patterns, baby-sitting pools and *kaffeeklatsch* circles, and as such it sustains an important flow of communication. It is not, however, apt to form polity beyond the "rules of the road," nor is it apt to represent its members in a larger collective. Its net product is small scale order, mutual aid, and friendship. Lack of a formal structure oriented to the collective needs and problems of the inhabitants facilitates the performance of minimal tasks, for the informal and usually unspoken norms relevant to the enclave allow for great flexibility and effective control of deviation. Such unformalized norms and unspecialized roles, however, are suitable only for a given routine, and preferably one requiring little precision. The self-ordering of the neighborhood is an ordering of routine interaction within wide tolerance limits. Thus, it is not formally related to any other level of spatially based organization; too small to be an administrative subunit, it is too informal to be a base for independent representation in a larger system. The principal contribution of the neighborhood to other organizational systems is one of communication; it is a site for conversational ferment.

The household is related to the larger local area through formal organizations sited in the locality. These are public structures and voluntary organizations related to them (PTA and school, or, the reverse, local business enterprise and the Kiwanis or Rotarians), or voluntary organizations based on other interests. The same activities that involve households in these area-wide (but selective and segmental) organizations, produce interest in the flow of communication through informal relationships and the local newspaper. Households differentially related to the local formal organizations gain a familiarity with the actors and dramas of the local community through their readership of the press and conversation with other participants.

The agencies of local government are also, in an important sense, segmental structures. In spite of the local government's conventional esthetic identification with a geographical space and all its population, it has very limited powers and duties and affects only a small part of the residents' vital activities. Still, with its control of legitimate force against all alike, it is different in kind from nongovernmental organizations.

The municipality is related to other levels of local organization through the congruence of fields of action (and convergence or conflict of interests) between the voluntary organizations and governmental agencies. Private organizations may act as representatives of community interests before the government; the same individuals frequently hold overlapping leadership roles within both government and private organizations; and the voluntary organization may become a political faction or party in local politics. Each kind of interrelation strengthens the argument that the local government is "truly representative of the community." Each has important consequences for the effectiveness of local government and the constraints upon it in dealing with local problems and issues.

There is, then, a large overlap between the members of voluntary organizations and those who participate in local government through voting, campaigning, and running for office. (So passive are the campaigns that the British term "standing for office" seems more appropriate.) The members of voluntary organizations are exceptionally sensitive to community news as reported in the local press, while the community press is given to extensive and frequent reporting of governmental affairs. As a consequence, the persons most active in local voluntary organizations are best informed with respect to the dramatis personae of community polity. Insofar as they are committed members of common interest organizations, they have additional reasons for following the trend of governmental events, for these frequently affect the ends and means of their group. While neighborhood structures involve a large proportion of the familistic neighborhood's population, this involvement hardly affects the polity of the residential community. Both the local area as a social system and the municipality involve a smaller proportion of the population, and one that is, to a large extent, composed of the same individuals.

Remembering the four levels of organization in the residential areas (household, neighborhood, residential community, and municipality), we can ask: what combinations of involvement in these structures are typical for metropolitan populations? How does the individual's life space exclude, or include and coordinate, participation in different organizational systems? Ninety per cent of the population falls into one of three "social types." These are the "isolates," the "neighbors," and the "community actors."[9]

Isolates are those who are literally disengaged from the organizational structure of their geographical space in the city; they operate as neighbors little if at all, and they belong to none of the voluntary organizations in the area. They are spiritual *émigrés* from the local community. They are poor voters; a majority of them have never voted in a local election. Though a few read the local newspaper, they read it chiefly for advertisements; they are ignorant and incompetent with respect to the local community's affairs, generally unable to name local personages of importance, and frequently not even aware that they live within a municipality that holds elections. While they are somewhat less apt to be college graduates than the average, many of them are highly educated and well paid—they simply do not opt for participation in the community.

Neighbors are those who are involved in the household and in the household's immediate social environment. Locally, they live in the small world of casual interaction and family friendships. They are disproportionately made up of younger families, and are most usually wives and mothers. Like the isolates, they participate at a low rate in local politics, and many of them have never voted. They are more likely, however, to read the local newspaper than the isolates, and somewhat more aware of the dramatis personae of the local area, but much of the reading simply supplies ammunition for neighborly gossip. For such individuals, the arena of social participation is limited: their path through the social space of the locality stops short at the bounds of the neighborly enclave.

Community actors are from all levels of education and occupation, are of all ages and both sexes. They are those who are involved in the local area, through membership in the local organizations, and are also a part of the communication flow of the area, through neighboring or reading the local paper for local news or both. They are likely (according to research carried out in St. Louis) to be somewhat better educated than the others and somewhat older on the average. However, they are as likely to be women as are the neighbors, and more so than isolates. Here, in fact, are the active clubwomen who run their share of the social organization in suburbia. But only half of them are women—men also participate vigorously. Community actors supply a disproportionately large part of the local electorate (about 70 per cent are local voters compared to 30 per cent of the isolates) and are by far the most knowledgeable type with respect to local personages, leaders, and the electoral contests of the area

Though the group of community actors are disproportionately made up of older families and people with higher educational and occupational levels, many persons with eighth grade and high school education are among them. In fact, community actors with an eighth-grade education are more active and competent in the community than isolates with college education, while the women of this social type are more competent than men of the other types. Though greater educational achievement and age may predispose people to become community actors, once they have made the commitments to the local community the organizational network itself involves and informs them.

Thus, most of the public affairs in the community of limited liability are carried on by a self-selected fraction of the population. When local voluntary organizations are spokesmen for corporate interests, it is for the community actors they speak. The latter are also disproportionately important in the outcome of local elections. But they are, in one sense, representatives of the total population. Insofar as they have the same household, neighborhood, and community commitments as those who are isolated or confine their lives to the neighborhoods, their actions stand for the whole community. They are virtual representatives. They may not always represent these interests in an unbiased fashion, but their organizational advantage assures them a strong voice, collectively, in the polity of the local area. They are a form of ruling class, a "Coxey's army" drawn from local businessmen and bureaucrats, small property owners, clubwomen, aspiring young lawyers, and the League of Women Voters.

The outcome of the various social types' participation in this social structure is the local area as a social fact, the "local community" insofar as one exists in the metropolis. Committed to the local area as a residence (though it is hardly a commitment to the death), the community actors strengthen their commitment through participating in the ongoing system. Their image of the local community is more definite than that of others, and they frequently invoke sacred values in defending its "character" as a place in which to live. Interacting more intensively with others as part of the community's organization, they also build up a strong primary dimension and the community of limited liability becomes, to some degree, a primary community for them, one standing upon hallowed ground.

But what of the others, those who stand aside in isolation and those whose local social world is limited to the neighborhood? We must remember that many of them are also objectively committed to the local area—through home ownership and all that implies, through children and all that implies. These commitments are shared with those who run the voluntary organizations—the Home Owners Association, the Improvement Association, the PTA. The nonparticipators benefit from the actions of their self-chosen representatives and frequently identify with them. In this fashion, they come to accept the polity, even as they share the image of their local area. Because there is a stable set of organizations to run the community, those who do not participate can nevertheless see and value the place as something more than a geographical site for family living. Like the average member of a labor union, they put little of themselves into their community most of the time, but when "the chips are down," when their image of the community is threatened, they may come out in droves to oppose change.

URBANISM, SUBURBANISM, AND
COMMUNITY ORGANIZATION

Life style, as the basis for similar interests, is a key
variable in producing these associational patterns and
locality groups that have been described. As residential enclaves are more consistently inhabited by familistic populations, interaction among households increases and the
neighborhood flourishes as a social system. Within a neighborhood at a given level of urbanism, however, variation
in neighboring is the result of variations in commitment
among individual households. Those with children, where
the woman does not work outside but is immersed in the
role of housewife and mother, are more involved, as are
those who own their homes.

Thus, the household is an important base for the organizational structure of an area, and similar households in
contiguity produce a multiplying effect, for they establish
the norms of interaction that are binding even upon people
who do not have children or own their homes. The latter
are surrounded by a social world, not a congeries of
buildings. But those who live a familistic life in a highly
urban neighborhood, in an apartment house surrounded
by childless couples, are hard put to maintain neighborly
relations and a community interest. The lack of opportunities results in an enforced isolation—there is nobody
available with whom the wife can gossip or the child
play.[10] In general, however, the concentration of similar
households geographically produces a fit between household needs and the organization of the area as a whole.

The same processes lead to similar relationships between
the urbanism or familism of a population and members in

local organizations. Commitment to the area increases steadily, as we move from the apartment house districts to the regions of the homeowners. And the commitment, which produces increased participation in neighborhood and local community organizations, also increases the value of communication relevant to the local area. Thus the degree of interaction in spatially defined groups varies directly with the familism of the population, and conversely with its urbanism.

The social types of local actors vary concurrently. Moving from the urban districts toward the familistic neighborhoods, from the central city's apartment houses to the outer wards and finally to the suburban tract developments, we find an increasing proportion of the adult population involved in both the small-scale order of the neighborhood and the larger local community, while isolates are a decreasing proportion of the total. In the highly urban districts, in contrast, the local community atrophies; the community paper degenerates into a "throwaway shopping news" subsidized by a supermarket; even the neighborhood shrinks and loses members, frequently to become no more than the casual greetings of those who live in the same apartment house.

## Social Rank, Ethnicity, and the Local Community

There are two other broad bases for social differentiation in the metropolitan population. Each is vividly reflected in the galaxy of neighborhoods that constitutes the city "at home." The first is *social rank*, which reflects the individual's educational achievement, his position in the division of labor of the society, and his share of the rewards in material goods and honor. The second is ethnicity, which reflects his placement in a social category of persons who differ physically or culturally, as a result of biological or social inheritance.

Each is the basis for differential treatment by other members of the society. This treatment is reflected in the distribution of home sites within the metropolitan grid of housing opportunities. People are segregated in neighborhoods among others of the same designated social rank and ethnic identity. There is thus the same social precondition, which makes the urbanism-familism continuum an important determinant of spatially defined social organization. Life style, however, is a much more important differentiator, for it points to the specific household necessities that are conducive to neighborhood and community participation. For this reason it has been discussed at length. We may conceive of social rank and ethnicity as modifiers, differentiating the locale as social fact *at each level of urbanism*. The three dimensions are independent however, and each has an effect upon community interaction.[11]

SOCIAL RANK

We have noted that higher occupation and education are marks of the community actors. This is congruent with the general finding that participation in voluntary organizations is more common among those of higher rank. Such participation strengthens the organizational network of the local area, with the consequence that, the higher the social rank of a residential area, the larger the proportion of the population who will be community actors. This does not mean that in the blue-collar neighborhoods the average person is an isolate.

What occurs, instead, is an increasing proportion of the social type we have called "neighbors." Although they may avoid the formal organizations of their community, persons of lower social rank do not avoid their neighbors any more than others do. We may say that, the lower the occupational and educational level, the smaller the scale of an individual's participation. This means, not that he is uninvolved, but that the radius of his interaction is shorter. Kinfolk and the small-scale world of the neighborhood grow relatively more important as we move through the urban landscape toward the low end of the social-rank continuum. In the familistic working-class neighborhoods we see, not the "faceless world of megalopolis," but men in shirt sleeves playing soft ball, groups of women gossiping on the porches, children swarming the streets, and vacant lots.[12]

However, as social rank declines the nature of the isolates changes. Those who avoid the local organizational structure in neighborhoods of higher social rank do so through choice; their worlds may be broad and rich, but the basic enterprises lie outside the local area. In the poor neighborhoods, however, the scale of participation for the isolate is limited indeed. His isolation in the neighborhood and community is complemented by segregation from the larger worlds of the metropolis. He is, in the extremely urban neighborhoods, the skid-row drifter, the alcoholic, the denizen of the flophouse and the "blind pig"—the homeless man. He does not choose isolation: he is disbarred from participation.[13] Less extreme but more common are the country boy or girl in the city, the aged who have outlived their families and jobs, the itinerant workmen. These are the people who figure large in such earlier pictures of the urban milieu as Harvey W. Zorbaugh's *The Gold Coast and the Slum*.[14]

An important consequence of variation in social rank is the changing proportion of the population that participates in the community of limited liability. As social rank declines and community actors become relatively less common, there is a greater concentration of control among a few people. Such persons are apt to be less representative of the total population, for the processes of self-selection increase discrepancies in education and occupation. Community actors in the neighborhoods of lower social rank are likely to be drawn from the occupationally involved—neighborhood businessmen, the employees of welfare bureaucracies and the schools, the local politicians. As the voluntary organization becomes less important in the system of the low-rank neighborhood, community actors tend to be self-interested men, as contrasted with the high-rank neighborhoods where clubwomen are important actors in the local drama. The smaller proportion involved results in a smaller proportion of informed bystanders who know, through friends and relatives, what is going on. The bias in representation produces latent suspicion and distrust of community leaders—for their interests are frequently seen as discordant with those of the ordinary man in a working class neighborhood. In the low-rank neighborhood there is a tendency toward the massified population at the community level, controlled by an informal machine relatively free to act within limits, but always potentially in trouble.[15]

ETHNICITY

Ethnic differentiation has two aspects, the cultural and the social. Cultural bases of ethnic status are those socially inherited patterns of norms (and resulting ways of living) differing radically from the publicly sanctified ways of the larger population. Such cultural variants are a result of the amalgamation of diverse peoples within a society of increasing scale. They are perpetuated by social learning in the family, the ethnic neighborhood, and the parallel institutions that immigrants and incapsulated survivors of conquest maintain or develop.

The second basis for ethnic differentiation rests, not upon the deviant culture of the ethnic enclave, but upon the differential treatment accorded one social category by the remainder of the society. Such differential treatment is manifest, in metropolitan society, in residential segregation. This, in turn, facilitates the development of parallel institutions (from corner groceries to political machines) that, in turn, perpetuate norms posited upon a basic difference in kind between the ethnic enclave and the remainder of the city.

The important ethnic groups for our purpose are those whose differential social position (whether through cultural variation or the social response) results in an organizational system that affects the local community. For this reason, segregation is the key to the effect of ethnicity on the local area. (Shevky originally entitled his index for this dimension a "segregation index."[16]) In contemporary American metropolitan areas the important ethnic populations are the foreign-born from Southern and Eastern Europe and their children, those whose religion differs radically from the American norm (chiefly Catholics and

Jews), and those whose pigmentation results in differential treatment by the remainder of the society (Negroes, Mexicans, and Puerto Ricans).

..*The Foreign-born.* Although the Immigration Acts of the 1920's shut off the flow of "foreigners" into the United States, there still persist enclaves in any large metropolis with distinctive cultures and positions in the rank order of honor. Little Tokyo, Chinatown, the Polish Corridor (or the ward in Cleveland whose boss annually puts on a "Nights in Budapest" for several thousand Hungarians) witness the continued social reality of the culturally variant local community.

In such places social rank and urbanism are affected by patterns of interaction brought from the old country. Beyond this, the neighborhood is greatly strengthened as an interactional scene by its competitive advantage—the native language is spoken here. It is strengthened also by the likelihood that relatives and friends will live close together, as compared with the vast distances of the metropolis.[17] (Firey tells of one apartment house in Boston entirely populated by *paisani* from the same village in Italy.) Segregation, in turn, provides a stable and predictable base for a rich maze of voluntary organizations; those brought from the old country, those developed for the purpose of bridging the gap between cultures, and those adopted from the dominant American society. Upon this base of parallel institutions, local political representation tends to be an ethnic monopoly, and participation in elections is stimulated by patriotism—whether for the country of origin or the underdog local enclave surrounded by strangers and enemies.

Such neighborhoods are usually in the central city,

and in the declining neighborhoods where the ethnic enclave "first landed in America." Their social rank tends to be low, for immigrants to America in the last decades typically have been manual laborers. They thus manifest a higher density of interaction at the local community level than other areas of similar rank and urbanism.

But such ethnic communities are declining in importance at a rapid rate. Many who attend the Nights in Budapest and march in the Columbus Day parade do so through nostalgia for the days that are gone. They drive in from the outlying neighborhoods where Adamowski, Cellebrizze, Tucker, and Daley live side by side with no questions asked. The children and grandchildren of the original settlers on the urban frontier still maintain an ethnic loyalty and they may vote for a "good name" in the larger elections of the city, county, state, and nation, but their local community is made up of those who, like themselves, are far from the ethnic home. In the high-rank neighborhoods of familistic populations, the ethnic traits barely linger. The dwellers in these areas behave like everybody else in local affairs, unless their religion deviates from the norm.[18]

*Catholics and Jews.* Although they are still excluded from a diminishing number of neighborhoods in the exurban fringe, neither native-born Catholics nor Jews are highly segregated in the contemporary metropolis. Their differential treatment at the hands of their fellow citizens is minor at most. Yet the persistence of cultural differences and the parallel institutions based upon religion have important effects upon the neighborhoods with high concentrations of either.

The Catholic ecclesia is more than a voluntary organization demanding a minimal participation. The good Catholic attends mass daily, ordinarily an early mass on weekdays; he sends his children to a parochial school maintained by the Church; he participates in such Church sponsored organizations as the Society of St. Vincent de Paul, the Sodalities, the Altar Societies, the Knights of Columbus. In short, the Catholic Church provides, in a way, a set of parallel institutions that can absorb all of the free time of the family; more important, many Catholics take seriously these participational opportunities.

The result is to create a degree of spatial concentration. The early mass requires that church be not too far distant, while the rule of thumb for location of elementary schools is that they be within a mile (walking distance) of the children's homes. Thus, the Catholic is concerned, when looking for a residential neighborhood, with the accessibility of his organizational network. Furthermore, when he moves into a neighborhood where Catholics live in numbers sufficient to justify a church and school, he is likely to find relatives in the same area. Religious endogamy tends to produce, not only religious uniformity among kinfolks, but kin among fellow communicants. Thus the neighborhood with a heavy concentration of Catholics may exhibit a higher degree of neighboring and of community organization than will others of similar social rank and urbanism. Concentration has results similar to segregation for the local area as a social system.[19]

Jews, like Catholics, are more likely to be descendants of the newer immigrants—with cultural bases in a transitional community, halfway between that of the Russian, German, or Polish, and that of the dominant American ethos. Though these roots may be far behind, the old folks are not; there is a tendency for Jewish households to move upward in social rank and to carry their ethnic past with them in the physical presence of their parents. The location of Synagogue and *Shule*, together with the limited living quarters available to them in the high-rank areas of suburbia, constitute a set of limits resulting in a combination of self-concentration and segregation for urban Jews. And, here again, religious endogamy brings together family, area, and church. This concentration perpetuates a dense interactional system, and, since Jews are usually in areas of middle to high social rank, a remarkable burgeoning of voluntary organizations. Some are specifically Jewish—B'nai B'rith and Daughters of Rachael; others are the usual service organizations.

*Negroes, Mexicans, and Puerto Ricans.* These are the latest migrants to the metropolitan areas of America; Negroes began to move in large numbers into New York and Chicago during World War I, while Mexicans were moving into Los Angeles and the other West Coast cities. Puerto Ricans began to come into New York in large numbers during World War II. Together, they constitute the only parallel to the massive immigrant populations of the earlier period.

As such they approximate, in many ways, the earlier forms of ethnic local community organization. Segregated, they provide the basis for a luxuriant development of parallel institutions; in fact, most commercial goods and services may be operated by fellow ethnics in the subareas where they dominate. The network of kinship is also coterminous with the spatial community. Thus, commercial enterprises, public facilities, kinship, and the ethnic community coexist within the local area. Upon this base is built a political structure permeated with the organizational influences of the residential community.

However, such activities are largely the perquisites of those with higher social rank while the great majority of these populations are of low social rank. Segregation blurs residential distinction by rank, forcing those who are so treated to live side by side in a limited area, whether or not their neighbors are those they would choose. The Negro ethnic enclave, for example, gives the impression of an immense amount of voluntary organizational participation, yet a very large proportion of Negroes in any metropolitan area belongs to no organization other than a church. Negro local areas in large cities range from the atomistic districts, where little organization exists beyond the bare governmental and commercial necessities, to areas in which the typical working-class neighborhood is reinforced by even greater interaction than usual, to a few familistic areas of middle social rank, which manifest a higher than average amount of local community organization. The mean, however, is the community where most people participate only in the neighborhood, and the self-selected few man the posts of "our community."[20]

### URBANISM AND ETHNICITY

Those who bear the distinctive marks of the ethnic are limited in their housing opportunities; one consequence is a correlation between urbanism and ethnicity. The segregated ethnic populations tend to live in the old, densely settled centers of the city—in tenements and row-houses or the discarded town houses of the departed prosperous. Since they do not live in these neighborhoods through choice, the consequence is frequently a disjunction between the life style of the population and the site of its everyday activities.

For this reason, segregated ethnic populations (the foreign-born, the nonwhites) who carry on in many ways a peasant or village form of local social life, typically exhibit a higher degree of neighborliness than would be expected for neighborhoods at their level of urbanism. Streets in the ethnic enclave are frequently replicas of the plazas in little Mexican towns, village markets in Puerto Rico, or the Negro quarters in small southern cities. Contrariwise, the layout of the site has important *limiting* effects upon the social life of ethnic localities. The urban peasant must contend with crowded quarters, unknown and heterogeneous neighbors, and the absence of public space for that communal gregariousness that he brings to the metropolis.

When, however, the limits associated with ethnicity recede, through the disappearance of language and cultural handicaps and increase of income, there is still a tendency for ethnic populations to be drawn to the highly urban neighborhoods. As they move upward in social rank they move from slum to gold coast. In part this is a continuation of the characteristic life they have been socialized to—life in the city's center (one can have a pious attachment to an urbane milieu as well as any other). In part it is also a reflection of the second and third generation's change of culture, from familism typical of the "old country" to an emphasis upon upward social mobility and consumership. The latter require a strict limitation or abnegation of children, unless income is higher than is usual among the children of immigrants.[21]

For those whose cultural equipment is not the cause of their residential concentration, however, acceptance of and accomplishment within the norms of the city only result in somewhat better quarters in the ghetto. Middle-class Negro families, committed to children and home, are still forced to live in tenements, public housing developments, or ancient brownstones, in the overcrowded areas of the central city. Their home is frequently in a state of siege, for they are surrounded by influences destructive to their precarious investment in a middle-class future for their children. The result is weakness in the leadership of social organization in the area, and isolation of the household.

## The Organizational Mosaic

This, then, is the pattern of the local communities within a metropolis. Populations more deeply committed to the local area as a place invest their time and energies locally, developing among a segment of the people who live there some of the attributes of a primary community. But as the nature of the residents changes, so does their average commitment—and so does the proportion who are deeply committed to the place. In the familistic suburbs the community of limited liability flourishes. When, however, we consider areas of low social rank, no matter how familistic their population they still include a large majority that participates only at the neighborhood level. The islands of the segregated are also deeply committed, though for reasons beyond their control or approval; their local area is frequently identified in discourse with the ethnic community itself, for the two tend to be coterminous.

Those who constitute the ruling class of the local community are a self-selected minority of the committed and the participation prone. Though they frequently represent the common interest in a biased fashion, yet they are the basis for the argument that the local community is democratic in its functioning. And this is not as absurd as it may sound; in a sense, the local community does represent the voice of *demos*. The community of limited liability approaches the earliest Greek definition of democracy. For the lottery that chose its representatives and officials, we may substitute the relatively random operations of the ballot in service clubs, the PTA, and the local municipality. It is true that all citizens' names do not get tossed into the organizational lottery; instead, we have the "eligibles," who have volunteered. They, however, may stand for the privileged class that constituted citizens in the Greek city-state.

As such, they stand for the total community as virtual representatives. And, indeed, community actors do not depart far from the averages in the suburban areas where the local community is most vigorous. A vote by the active participators is probably not too bad a sample of general opinion, if that opinion were activated through social involvement and informed through participation. The community actors are, in this sense, that functionally specialized random selection of the residential population that mans the posts in the civic table of organization, creating in the process the local community.

# THE
# URBAN
# POLITY

From the mosaic of local community organization emerges much of the structure of the metropolitan electorate. From the pattern of the people who inhabit the sprawling metropolitan complex, varying in life style, ethnicity and social rank, derives the local community organization and the distribution of social types. In familistic areas community actors increase and isolates decrease, while with declining social rank the proportion of community actors decreases and neighbors take their place in the distribution of types.

But we have seen that the community actors are most likely to vote and most politically competent as citizens. Participating in the voluntary organizations of the community, they take part in the continual process of defining issues and organizing public opinion. Having an opinion, they exercise it in the balloting. Thus, the distribution of the voters and the informed in the metropolis tends also to be a distribution of those with a greater than average commitment to a local area as a community and a valued place. These parochial interests are not necessarily in conflict with commitments to a larger political entity. Just as the person who is engaged at the residential community level may also be a good neighbor, so may the community actor be in many respects a metropolitanite, an actor in the metropolitan community. Though the people who participate at different levels in the organizational structure of the metropolis are not necessarily the same, there is no inherent contradiction in multilevel participation; some are involved at *every* level. They are the organizational binders of the spatially defined social group.

### THE COMMUNITY OF LIMITED LIABILITY
### IN CENTRAL CITY AND SUBURBS

The central city ordinarily encompasses the bulk of the highly urban neighborhoods for it inherits its physical structure from the paleotechnic city of the railroad. As such, it includes most of the neighborhoods of the very poor and those in which the culturally variant and segregated populations live. A large proportion of the central city, including most of the inner area, is not conducive to the existence of powerful local communities. Instead, many areas have a preponderance of isolates and neighbors. The suburbs, however, with few of the very poor, few of the segregated ethnics, and a very large proportion made up of home-owning, familistic populations, are the elysian fields of community action. The importance of the Junior Chamber of Commerce, the Lions and the Rotarians, the American Legion and the League of Women Voters, is further accentuated by a separate political organization—the suburban municipality.

A similar (or even smaller) proportion of the citizens vote in suburban local elections than in those of the central city. Though suburban citizens are much more apt to say they think most local elections are important, they do not, in many cases, follow through at the polls. Whether the election in question is for school-board member or mayor of the municipality, a smaller proportion of the eligibles will turn out to vote in the suburbs than will do so in the central city. Some have argued that this is because they are satisfied with their "virtual representation" but powerful evidence indicates this may not be the case. For the residents of the suburbs are, in a much larger proportion of the cases, in no position to decide: in one study 20 per cent of those eligible to vote in municipal elections did not know it, and the same was true of 30 per cent where school board elections were involved.[1]

Within the central city and suburbs alike, community actors are more likely to know the political score and to vote in local elections. There are, however, fewer community actors and more isolates in the central city wards, since the highly urban low-rank populations are less conducive to a strong organizational system at the locality level. Still, the central city electorate is more widespread than that of suburbia. How are we to explain this anomaly?

Organizationally, the government and politics of the central city are on a much greater scale than those of the suburban municipalities. Comprising only one municipal government and school district, the "city" consumes a large budget, employs thousands of persons, and deals with decisions representing basic policy for the metropolitan region as a whole. In the suburbs local government is small in scale and concerns itself, in many cases, with small events. If the cake is cut into enough pieces they become so small that nobody gets much of a taste of patronage, power, or glory.

Furthermore, the elections for officials of the central city are, in cities of metropolitan scale, highly partisan. Democrats and Republicans contend by party label (although the incumbents in most American cities have been overwhelmingly Democratic for years) and partisan identification with the national political moiety can be mobilized for local conflict. Contrariwise, the nonpartisanship of local governments in the suburbs is another way of discouraging interest in elections.

As a result of these two conditions, the large-scale, partisan government of the central city automatically becomes "news." It is invested with the drama resulting from continuous coverage by the mass media, and the spotlights of the metropolitan newspapers, television and radio, shine upon the actors in the local scene. They in turn loom large in the formation of the urban polity, developing followers and mass images.

In this respect the government of the greater urban polity is "closer to the people"—they see its symbols with their morning coffee. Consequently, although there are more local isolates in the central city, they nevertheless become involved in the electoral contests for city-wide office. They belong, in some cases, to the voluntary organizations spanning many local areas (unions, ethnic organizations, church-connected groups, and the like) and their media of communication are city-wide—the daily press and television. For them the total city takes the place of the local community. For others, there is little connection between the "parapolitical structure" of organizations and politics; they may be the isolated mass men whose social world is unified only in print, or they may be the political indifferents of the low-rank neighborhoods, voting only as clients of the machine.[2]

We may make an instructive comparison between such urban voting patterns and suburban voting for county officials. In these elections about the same proportion of suburbanites usually vote as do urbanites for municipal elections in the central city. This is because the county government in the metropolitan suburbs is also a large-scale government, and it usually has partisan elections. National parties, trumpeting national war cries, lend a glamour and partisan interest to the contest for offices as diverse as those of county assessor, coroner, sheriff, and highway engineer, as well as councilman or superintendent. In consequence, county elections are given wide coverage by the metropolitan dailies and other mass media, while the local branches of national parties struggle to get out the vote.

The small-scale community of limited liability in the suburbs does not have the "box office appeal" that major government manifests. Staying close to home, operated by amateurs and part-time politicians (whose local working day begins after they return from their jobs in the central city) the suburban political community has been overlooked or rejected by a substantial proportion of its citizenry.

### CITIZEN RELATIONS WITH GOVERNMENT

Participation in elections is not, however, the only measure of citizen interest in, and access to, local government. Those who insist that the small municipality brings government "closer to the people" say that the citizens have more access to their elected representatives because they are made up of friends and neighbors. They not only have the opportunity to speak up and be heard through their membership in voluntary organizations, but can also go directly to the man they elected. This is facilitated by a bureaucratic hierarchy that is foreshortened as a result of the smaller organizational unit.

And indeed, in the recent study of citizen-government relations carried out by the Metropolitan St. Louis Survey, this was true. Here, if anywhere, in a suburban complex with ninety-six municipalities having a median size of less than one thousand, government should be close to the people. And, compared with the central city residents, a much larger proportion of the citizens who felt like complaining about their governmental services did so. The suburban citizen as client had approached the bureaucracy that provided his services in a majority of the cases where he was dissatisfied.[3]

When he approached the governmental machinery he was much more likely to go to a specific person whom he had elected, while the central city resident went to a clerk in a faceless bureaucracy. The fragmentation of suburban government provides a veritable army of elected functionaries who are available and sensitive to the complaints of their clients and constituents. The higher average educational and occupational level of the suburbanites is reflected then, not in greater competence and participation in local electoral contests, but in what might be called "the gripe function" of democratic government.

After they had griped, however, the suburban complainants had no better chance of finding their situation remedied than did those in the central city. After all, such complaints arise from conditions that are often beyond the control of the governmental official. (In the suburbs, they are frequently beyond the very limited resources of the entire municipality.) Letting off steam may be conducive to emotional peace; it is effective in governmental action only when organized into blocs of votes. This rarely occurs spontaneously anywhere in the metropolitan community.

### LOCAL COMMUNITY LEADERSHIP

The close relationship between local voluntary organizations and government on one hand and local business and government on the other, reported by the local community paper, allows the resident of the familistic area more familiarity with local leaders and personages. Though a great many cannot name even one leader, those who are community actors can usually name one and frequently know of a dozen local leaders. In the highly urban areas, however, a much smaller proportion can name any local leader; when they do so, the leaders they name are likely to be political actors. While in the sub-urban community municipal officials loom large in the perceived local leadership, in the apartment-house districts of the central city almost all leaders named are politicians. They are local representatives to the greater polity. The local councilman, committeeman, or county superintendent, is seen as their local leader by those who live within the urban areas of the city.[4]

The partisan nature of elections in the central city, together with the large-scale powers and perquisites of government there, form the basis for the urban political apparatus—"the machine." Capitalizing upon the loyalties of the residents to their national political party, staffed with government employees and the politically aspiring, the big city machine weaves together the interests of the familistic communities of the outer city, the workingmen's neighborhoods, and the ethnic-identified populations. Built upon precinct and ward, it approximates the neighborhood and the local community, and the total population has available to it opportunities for participation in, and representation before, the urban polity.

As we have seen, most urbanites do not take advantage of these opportunities. In the city itself the principle of limited liability results in a self-selected sample of the population that "loves politics" and frequently makes a good thing of them. Traditionally, this sample has emphasized and overemphasized the ethnic proportion of the population, for the segregated ethnic communities constitute dependable blocs of support within the electorate, while politics has been one of the early channels of upward mobility opened for ethnics. In all kinds of neighborhoods, however, the party clubs are small in membership, and

most of the electorate avoids those organizational housekeeping chores resulting in the selection of the candidates
for whom they can vote. Controlling the primary, the
"machine" does not need to control the general election
—and usually does not do so. It wins in a landslide through
the inertia of national party loyalties, guided by the party
label in local elections.[5]

## The Governmental Dichotomy of the Metropolis

The structure of local government in the suburbs is
horizontal and diffuse. A maze of small governmental units
organizes the suburban sprawl for those unavoidable common tasks that only government can perform. On the average, these suburban units are so small, however, that all
leaders are "the same height," and not very tall. No parlia-
ment coordinates these dozens (or hundreds) of towns,
cities, villages, and townships. They coexist as equals, each
controlling the powers assigned by the state constitutions
to the municipality.

There is a certain amount of fit between this governmental network and the local community structure of
suburbia. The residential community of limited liability
reinforces the small municipality. For one thing, agreement on the community image legitimatizes its separatism
from other areas and the larger polity. For another, the
community actors create a network of relations between
the municipality and the participational structure of
neighborhoods and voluntary organizations. The commitment of the residential population to the specific local-

ity, through home ownership and the investment of their children's future in local schools and neighborhoods, supports this separation. Government is a "Chinese wall" protecting the character of the people in the neighborhoods, the character of school and school children their children will know, and their investment in property.

These interests are common to most of the members of each suburban political community. They are bases for consensus and this consensus is reinforced by the effects of social homogeneity. Most of the municipalities have few ethnic members; they are inhabited by those who have opted for familism and the home-centered life; and, because of their small size and the "tract" pattern of residential building, they are of similar social rank. Thus, it is easy to identify with the people of one's suburb—they are much like you. Schism in such a community occurs rarely if at all; there is little to split and fight about. The strength of the suburban political leader is that of one who stands for a constituency "just like himself" on relevant matters.

In contrast, the central city is a vertical organizational structure, one with a highly concentrated executive having great powers over the every-day housekeeping tasks of the metropolis as well as the direction of its future development. Because it encompasses a wide range of population types, varying in social rank, ethnicity, and life style, and because its basic decisions affect differentially those in different social positions, the effective consensus is forever changing with the composition of the population and its resulting interests.

The weakness of the local community as a social fact produces a certain fit with its governmental structure. In the highly urban apartment-house districts the precinct committeemen and the ward club staffed by professionals carry out the specialized tasks of politics for which there are few alternative structures available. With their occupational stake in the outcome of future elections, they make it their business continually to sound out public opinion and fit the party's nominees to it (though the tolerance limits may be very wide). Like national parties, they search for issues to place on the agenda. They are sensitive to problems of the social segments who make up the city, and to the ongoing affairs of the urban neighborhoods.

In the polity of the central city, representation tends to be by interest group as reflected in the heterogeneous galaxy of residential areas making up the city's ward structure. Just as the central city politicians use the national party allegiances to organize electoral opinion, so they use the strategy of the national party in getting out the vote. Ethnic heterogeneity produces the balanced ticket with a representative of each major ethnic group present. Variation in social rank results in the selected candidate for the "silk-stocking district" and the selected candidate for "back of the yards." The people of the central city vary in interests, not so much by commitment to different areas as "hallowed ground" as by commitment to social segments with which they share a common fate.

Thus, the electorate of the central city is in many ways the national electorate writ small. However, it is the national electorate biased heavily in favor of urbanized neighborhoods, neighborhoods of foreign-born, Negroes, Puerto Ricans, Mexicans—neighborhoods of the blue-collar worker and the working girl. These populations support the Democratic ticket in the national elections and their alignment in the partisan elections of the central city reflects this over-all loyalty. Labor unions, the NAACP and the Urban League, the Sons of Garibaldi and Kosciusko, and others, including (not least) the professionals of the Democratic Party, are the corporate actors that contend for patronage, power, profit, and the control of the polity in the central city. Still, to gain a spectacular percentage, the central city politician must also appeal to the "outer wards," the familistic neighborhoods much like those of suburbia in population and social structure. Thus, the central city polity does represent most of urban America—but in a biased fashion.

ALIENATION VERSUS THE
TRIVIALIZATION OF POLITICS

Though the politics of the central city may be made more immediate to the citizens by a favored position on the front page of the metropolitan daily, so large is the structure and so distant the few leading figures that most people simply have no concrete involvement in politics. Their identification of politics with corruption, some enemy ethnic enclave, or unsavory alliances between opportunists and criminals, tends to produce a degree of alienation from the political and governmental processes. The large scale of government and the size of the stakes professionalizes politics. The professionalization of politics, in turn, results in a tendency toward the "state of the masses." Whether they are the urbane residents of the gold coast or the semiliterate recent migrants living precariously in the slums, the highly urban populations seldom participate in the organizations that represent their districts in the urban polity.

The electoral importance of the highly urban neighborhoods, in turn, shifts the general relationship between citizen and government in the central city toward that of a client and his agency. The familistic neighborhoods participating in the larger electorate and governmental structure are outweighed (just as the Republican members of a great city's council are consistently outvoted). The particular interests of their local community are apt to fare poorly against the interests of the broad segments of society —ethnics, unions, the party organization—that are the basis of political control. This, in turn, reinforces their alienation from politics, for these neighborhoods of nonethnic homeowners feel they are on the outside looking in at a city run for the others.

In the suburbs, however, the political process suffers from trivialization. Many citizens have never paid any attention to their local elections, and frequently it is hard to find anyone who will stand for election to public office. (In St. Louis County a substantial number of municipalities had no contested offices in the elections of 1957, while in several small municipalities *no one at all* would run for office. In the latter cases the hapless incumbents were obliged, by law, to continue in office!)

This trivialization stems in large part from the small scale of municipal government in the suburbs. Not only is the amount of money collected and disbursed small, but the very nature of decisions that can be made is trivial. Most of the major problems confronting the suburbanite cannot be solved through his municipality. Indeed, such municipalities are frequently, by tacit consent, "do nothing governments." Incorporated to prevent annexation by the central city or a neighboring suburb, they stand for a *status quo* based upon the image of the residential neighborhoods. However, these governmental enclaves are "worms in the body politic," as Hobbes would put it. They cannot approach such problems as area-wide traffic congestion, inadequate drainage and sewerage, economic development and planning. Neither their governmental powers nor the consensus upon which they rest will permit such ventures into polity. But they can block their performance by other governments.

Many citizens of the central city are alienated from the processes of government and have no responsible role in politics; they leave it to the "professionals," fulfilling their own political expectations by voting and exercising the "gripe function." The suburban citizen is not alienated from his municipal government but he is frequently uninterested in it. At one extreme, in the high-rank municipalities, he delegates a polity without issues to the professional manager, watched closely by the self-selected leaders who sit on the council; at the other extreme a "shadow government" furnishes part-time policy and collects taxes, relying upon volunteer fire departments, the county facilities, and low taxes as a substitute for government.

# The Metropolitan Area
# as a "Power Structure"

There have always been many Americans who prefer to believe that power in the local community is tightly organized in the hands of a few persons who represent "the interests." Perhaps this is a rural survival, for in the small town there is some evidence of consistent domination by those who control land, credit, and wealth.[6] Such an image can be easily transplanted to the city, where the mass media emphasize a few large-scale images connected with the polity, ignoring the supporting organizations and their dependence upon the citizens. The average urbanite, viewing these affairs from a great social distance, can easily believe that a small circle of the powerful exists and runs the city.

This image of the metropolitan area's power structure usually relies upon the assumption that local government is merely the executive committee of the bourgeoisie and the politicians hired hands of those who control the massive resources of the corporations. Floyd Hunter has documented such an image for Atlanta, Georgia, ending up with a list of a small number of people who are said to run things.[7] Such studies are based upon "perceived influence" and they suffer from a curious solipsism. For, if the notion of monolithic power structure is diffused through the society, and if one approaches the study of power by asking people what they think occurs, he is very apt to document a myth—held sincerely and even fervently by his subjects, but quite likely to be as far from the truth as any other proposition about society upon which most people agree.[8]

There is a touching naïveté in this faith, shared equally by left, right, and center. The ideologues of the left, confused and bemused by social transformations never posited in their theories, cling to the notion that *some* things do not change. The businessmen of main street have a vested interest in the image: it emphasizes their prestige and power and reinforces their own notions of who the first class citizens are, and what interests are legitimate. The vulgarized radicalism that has permeated American thinking leads diverse people to find reassurance in a conspiracy theory of local government.

When, however, careful scholars investigate the way key *decisions* come about in the metropolis, they find neither the dominance of business interests nor the simple order assumed in the myth. Recent studies of New York, Philadelphia, Boston, St. Louis, Chicago, and Syracuse all present striking evidence that there is no simple structure, hierarchical and monolithic, deploying the power of the ruling classes and running the city (Kaufman and Sayre, Reichley, Baltzell, Norton Long, Long and Greer, Banfield, Banfield and Meyerson, Wilson, Freeman and associates).[9] Instead, the businessmen are seen as limited in their influence, poorly organized and internally divided in their interests—frequently, in short, captives or pawns in a game where they do not hold the decisive advantage and frequently do not understand the play. Metropolitan politics, a continual interplay of other interests, has been given the felicitous name of "an ecology of games" by Norton Long. For the single pyramidal structure of control in the city, he substitutes a pluralistic political world where, like a continual game of musical chairs, the chief actors change positions as the issues revolve.

The myth of the economic ruling class makes two major assumptions about the metropolitan community in large-scale society. It assumes that there is a great commitment by businessmen to the fate of the local community, resting upon a great commitment of their corporate wealth and power. It also assumes that they have the instrumental ability to affect the local polity in the light of their corporate interests, to "call the shots" as the community agenda is formulated and acted upon.

Perhaps at one time, in the early decades of expanding scale, these assumptions held true. Perhaps, when the various large cities were all important headquarters of massive corporations, the latter were such citizens as elephants among chickens. Certainly today both assumptions can be questioned. Mills has pointed out the consequences of increasing scale for the corporation's commitment to the local area. Increasing scale means corporate merger, and the great and powerful corporate citizens in the community of yesterday are, today, branch plants of national organizations. The consequences, from the point of view of the career bureaucrats who now manage these plants, have been spelled out by Norton Long in detail; the effects of such changes upon the polity in a "satellite city" have been investigated by Schulze. Baltzell has demonstrated the diminishing concern of Philadelphia gentlemen for the local community, as their own interests focus more upon New York and Washington and they become part of a national upper class.[10]

The manager of the branch plant is primarily a citizen in his national corporation, and his lodestar is company headquarters. To his own career, local affairs are relatively unimportant. His aim is to pursue the corporation's advantage (and thus his own) as quietly as possible, letting the sleeping community dogs lie. He makes a one-way gamble if he gets "involved" in local affairs—it can profit him little, and it can hurt him a great deal. His strategy is the limited one of protecting the company's public relations and trying to keep at least a consultative status and a veto on those issues that could cost the company dearly. And so his role is usually defined by headquarters. Proconsular in his position, each major commitment to the local community must be reviewed by his superior and every cent of his war chest accounted for. Powerful as he may be in the imaginations of local citizens, his power is usually the passive force of a bureaucratic instrument, part of a larger social machine.

In the corporation headquarters city matters may have another weight, for here the autonomy and the power coexist. But in the headquarters of a national or international organizational network, immediate local affairs usually appear trivial. In the light of the corporation's function, the chief advantage of *this* city, *this* community, may be no more than the residential preferences of the top staff and a relatively minute investment in a building or two. The geography of large-scale bureaucracy is quite different from that of the geography textbooks. Organizational space supersedes geographical space for most purposes.

So much for the real giants of American business and industry; they are, in large degree, neutral actors in the local community polity. However, there are other firms that are inevitably committed to a given city. The metropolitan newspapers are nontransferable assets, and their fate is linked to that of their city. So also are the local banks (particularly in states that forbid branch banking) and the closely related real-estate companies. Public utilities are earth-bound, their fortunes inextricably involved with those of the metropolitan community as a whole. Retail merchants also have, in plant and clientele, assets that have value in this city, but perhaps in no other. The civic leaders of Chicago or St. Louis, Boston, Los Angeles,

or Cleveland, are drawn from the managerial and ownership ranks of these businesses (and such businesses are
apt to be locally owned). They are committed: their liability is greater—they have nowhere else to go. They are,
then, the chief corporate actors of business in the local
community.[11]

But there is a second assumption underpinning the
classic myth of community control: the committed economic powers have the ability to call the tune for local
government. Again, this may once have held, in smaller
cities of a smaller-scale society. But in a society where
the decisive actors of formal government are elected by
the citizens, such political actors would have to share either
a common normative system with voters and businessmen,
or else have great freedom from the opinions of the voters
and a great commitment to businessmen. The mechanisms
assumed are usually (1) gross manipulation of votes and
voters, insuring freedom from the electorate and its interests, and (2) the need for money from businessmen,
for elections, bribery, and the personal income of politicians (for an extreme statement see "Plunkitt of Tam-
many Hall"[12]).

These conditions certainly do not obtain in the contemporary metropolitan area. Neither the amateur governments of the suburbs nor the large-scale government of
the central city can disregard the perceived interests of
a majority with impunity. The increasing education, income, and occupational level that have affected all of the
diverse populations of the city have forced an increasing
emphasis upon issues of the community that are real to
the residents. The absorption of the children of immigrants into the middle ranks of the familistic neighbor-

hoods has weakened the power of the "ethnic name." Such devices as voting machines have made ballot-box stuffing increasingly dangerous. These changes in the nature of elections and the electorate have shifted the strategies of political victory from the simple disbursement of money to manipulation of the local branch of the national political party—for it is the party label that wins. As this occurs, the power of the businessman's campaign donation has shrunken proportionately. While bribery is undoubtedly still effective in some cases, it should always be remembered that the politician, like any organizational actor, usually will put the conditions for job security and progress in the job above everything else. Bribery by business would be defined as "selling out" to the enemy. In short, the businessman cannot often affect an official's political success one way or the other.

The weakness of the businessman in politics is also partly a result of the massive shift in residence within the governmentally bifurcated metropolis. The population that has moved outward has included the great majority of what was, once, the Republican basis of strength in the central city. The familistic, nonethnic, higher-rank residents have moved to the suburbs, leaving a pathetic remnant of Republican councilmen to represent the two-party system in most great American cities.

Along with the Republican voters, the leaders of the business community have gone to the suburbs. Equally important is the loss of the middle-level cadres of the middle class—the aspiring junior executives and young lawyers, the educated and politically inclined club women, the small businessmen. These are the people who could constitute an effective organizational middle class for the electoral contests of the city. Their disappearance from the scene leaves those economic leaders who remain in the city (in the town houses and private streets of yesterday) far up in the organizational stratosphere, with no links to the mass of voters. And the latter are, increasingly, union members, ethnics, and confirmed Democrats.

The central city has become a one-party state, and the party is one that business leaders, as good Republicans, would find unattractive even if they were welcome in it. The issues of the central city polity—public housing, aid for the handicapped, slum clearance, improvements in race relations, aid to dependent children—are not the issues close to the heart of their national party. Nor are the solutions hit upon any more welcome; federal aid in massive quantities, increasing taxes upon property and business enterprise, subsidy of mass transit—such policies do not sit well with the ideologist of Main Street.

Yet this civic agenda and these solutions are inescapable conditions within which he must live, for his treasure and his home are separated by more than space; they are separated by political boundaries and social milieus. The owners of the great investments downtown are committed willy-nilly to the policies of the central city with respect to taxation, urban redevelopment, highway location, building construction regulations—yet they are often unable to influence that polity. The classic dichotomy between wealth and numbers is accentuated by the political schizophrenia of the business elite; the issues that concern their basic occupational interests are settled in the central city's chambers of government and at the polls of the urban wards, while they are citizens of small suburban municipalities.

As citizens of the toy government in suburbia, they are indeed influential. Under the guise of a nonpartisan government, the municipalities in areas of high social rank are usually conservative. They stand pat with a definition of themselves as business operations controlled by a board of directors and its chairman, administered by an appointed manager. Such a government is remarkably congruent with the businessman's ordinary occupational milieu, and within the limited powers and electorate of the upper-class suburb he is an involved and participating citizen. It is a good solution to the problem of governing residential enclaves of homogeneous, nonethnic, middle-class Americans. The trouble is that this is not the business leader's major governmental problem in contemporary cities. His overweening problem is the concentration of his wealth in a "foreign country" ruled by the Democrats, and for this his "board of directors" government is no solution at all.

For the central city, large in scale, heterogeneous in population, diverse and conflicting in its interests, demands a polity that takes its nature into account. The norms of efficiency and economy (with their hidden assumptions about what is important) are subordinated to the need for growth, rescue operations, adjustment to change—in short, the reorganization of the community to fit the changing demands of the citizens. Large central cities mirror the conflicts and dilemmas of large-scale society in their politics.

The disappearance of the opposition, however, has had profound effects upon the control structure of the central city. In the security of its control the Democratic Party can choose the officials of the city government with great freedom, since a Republican victory is highly un-

likely. The party, however, suffers some of the effects
V. O. Key has spelled out for the Democratic Party
in the South. That is, the true arena where office is won
becomes the party primary, in which party discipline is
continually exposed to dangerous onslaughts.[13]

Ironically, victory has disorganized the central city
Democratic machine in a way that adversity could never
do. The lack of a common enemy has dissolved the discipline of battle. At the same time, the preconditions for
"tight" control of the primaries are disappearing. Civil
service and federal welfare agencies cut down the patronage that can be used to water the fields. The solid wards
of the uneducated ethnics who will do as they are told,
the "mattress wards" that can be bought, become a small
minority of an electorate whose whole relation to politics
shifts with its rising educational level and greater income.
The primaries are threatened by the friends and neighbors
vote, as in the one-party South.

This dissolution of the party is camouflaged by the
continued importance of "Democrats" in the government
of the city. But the armature of the party organization is,
more and more, the official bureaucracy of government—
the team of incumbents with its tremendous advantage in
publicity—while the party clubs diminish in importance.
They will continue to exercise some influence, as long as
the forced communities of Negroes and other ethnics are
major parts of the central city electorate, but their nature
will change as these wards grow more concerned with
their own particular interests. These interests are most
tangibly served by the incumbents, through appointments,
ordinances, and the distribution of public works. The net
result of the Democratic victory in the central city has

been the strengthening of the incumbent officials and a merging of latent and manifest political leadership, of party roles and governmental roles.

In the newer metropolitan areas, such as the California cities, the result has been a sort of nonpartisanship among elected officials. There the bases of party control, in unlimited patronage and the massive votes of the segregated wards, have never been strong enough to sustain a real machine. The heritage of formal nonpartisanship has blurred party lines, and the central city has evolved a kind of rule based almost entirely upon the party of the incumbents. For these reasons such cities may be, not deviants, but forerunners of the future government in all of the larger central cities.

Whatever the process by which he is first elected, the central city mayor, through the continual dramatization of the mass media, develops a very great staying power. He becomes, to an appreciable degree, "above his party." His personal following then allows him a degree of autonomy from the party, which he can exploit to separate himself from the public images of crooked politics. (Thus, the anomalous situation in which the mayor of a great city renowned for corruption in local government can be considered innocent of that corruption.) The mayor, however, still has a very great control over the administrative branches in most city governments, and his logistic advantages permit him to dominate his party. The result is a tendency toward the coalescence of his role and that of party boss.

The mayor, however, does not act with unlimited freedom. Although he can press to the limits with formal and informal directives and vetos, he can do so only at a price.

This price varies by issue, for the corporate interests involved shift as the bone of contention changes, from an increase in taxes to a fair employment ordinance, from an urban renewal project to a new public hospital. But there will always be interested parties. They range from other publicly elected officials to parts of the Democratic Party organization, from a social segment of the voters such as Negroes or Jews to the chamber of commerce, from powerful members of the national party hierarchy to influential leaders of the local business community. In any case, the newspapers will mirror the struggle, sketch in the protagonists, report their speeches, and lay the basis for opinion formation. And, frequently, the newspapers themselves are key protagonists.

The mayor comes to stand, then, for the reconciliation of the diverse and conflicting interests of the city in a single polity. Standing above the factions in his public image (and frequently in fact) he is forced to consider the common interest of the city as a whole. Though each interest group can press without inhibition, his role is not that of an interest-group representative. He may even become, in many cases, an enemy of his own party organization, for his role in the functioning organization of the city is so demanding that he tends to sacrifice the tactical advantages of the party machine to the necessities of good administrative practice as he understands it. Sooner or later the central city mayor is apt to decide that "good government is good politics." And it is, for him. It allows him to rise above his party, to desert the boys in the back room, to capture the imaginations of the suburbanites as well as the heterogeneous denizens of the urban neighborhoods—to become a symbol of the metropolitan community.

His role places him astride the divided metropolitan area like a colossus; it is the major political position in the metropolitan community as a whole. In suburbs and central city alike, the large minority of the residents who perceive an area-wide leadership will concentrate their nominations upon political actors—and the chief actor is the mayor of the city. In the same way as city government in general, he acts on a large scale and he is a hero of the mass media. Furthermore, today he is everywhere concerned with the disjunction between his rights and his duties. So many of the central city's problems are inevitable concomitants of change originating far beyond its boundaries that he, who is responsible for them, is painfully aware of the consequences of the governmental dichotomy for the area as a whole. He is necessarily a "metropolitan citizen." (In the recent campaign for a metropolitan district government in St. Louis the mayor of the central city was the chief authority respected by the citizens, even in the suburbs. He was known and his opinion on the proposed change was known, by a majority of those who voted.)[14] Of all the evidence that the metropolitan area is, in some sense, a single social and political community, this generalized importance of the central city's politics and, particularly, its mayor, is the most impressive.

## The Municipal Polity

Thus, local government in the metropolitan area does not approach the image of the monolithic power structure at many points. Instead of a pyramidal structure, controlled at the top by the representatives of economic interests, we find a pluralistic world of corporate citizens contending for power. The veto groups range from the corporation whose assets are captive to the polity of the central city, on one hand, to the Puerto Rican wards or the suburban municipalities on the other.

This contention occurs within a framework dominated by the political organization—and in the central city, that organization is the local wing of the Democratic Party. But because of recent political transformations the governmental personnel are generally dominant. The team of the incumbents, especially the big city mayor, are the key actors. Among them, the heads of the giant bureaucracies loom large. They move consistently and continuously toward autonomy, security, and expansion. Fire, education, police, health, and other specialized agencies become organizational empires outlasting any given administration.[15] Their professional commitments and relative freedom from party apparatus allow a genuine concern with universal norms. The mayor's autonomy allows him to concern himself also with the welfare of the city as a whole. The two kinds of actor, in combination, stand for political virtue and expertise. These attributes are frequently respected, in turn, by business representatives who see in a "clean" and professional mayor only another executive like themselves.

Big business has few "trading cards" for the game of big city politics. It can exercise real power only at the top, for it lacks the troops to contend in the electoral domain. Its chief political force derives from (1) bargaining rights due to party control elsewhere, in the State House or in Washington; and (2) the potency of the newspapers, which are usually Republican in their ideology and which are big business in their own right. As distinguished from "power," businessmen have influence insofar as their opinion, as experts and as folk heroes of American middle-class society, matters to the mayor and his team. Evidence indicates that, in certain respects, it matters a great deal. For the big city mayor, emancipated from his machine allies, behaves much like a respectable, suburban, middle-class citizen.

In the multitudinous municipalities of suburbia, a power structure does frequently exist. But it is a structure very democratic in its nature. The social homogeneity of the citizens, their equality in social honor and resources, their common image of the local community—all these result in a self-selected sample that holds the offices of government. This oligarchy overemphasizes the role of businessmen, for their prestige is transferable to the political realm in a community that accepts the ethos of Main Street as definitive. They often produce a "clean" government, run by a manager, supported by a good government caucus party whose ward-heelers are members of the League of Women Voters.

Within these frameworks of control, the everyday business of governing a metropolis proceeds. In the central city the organizational subsegments of government are social machines organized as bureaucracies, governed by explicit norms and informed with professional codes. The public administrator and the jurisprudent, the specialist in police administration and the certified public accountant, are culture carriers who rationalize (and disenchant) the jungle of corruption and power that so fascinated Lord Bryce. For party conflict is substituted competition among the "different branches of the service," the lobbying of special interest groups and the struggle of party chieftains (who are usually elected officials) for the succession.

In the suburban municipalities the management-oriented administrator is also frequently dominant as is the city manager of a small city. He works patiently within the circle of his amateur politicians, trying to educate them to the necessities of operating a going concern (which the municipality is) within a context of public responsibility and visibility (which a business firm is not). In towns without professional managers, the reason for their absence is usually anemia of the fisc; though some corruption occurs in such places, it is much more likely to be the incompetence of the officials that strikes the observer.

The sum of these arguments then, is this. No polity can embrace the total metropolis: too many legally autonomous structures are in being and there is always the dichotomy between central city and suburbia. Nor is a powerful, consistent, and continuous program of change likely in a central city. The mayor has strength, but chiefly to arbitrate among competing bureaucracies, business interests, ethnic minorities, and party organizations. Banfield describes Chicago's major issues for a two-year period; the majority resulted in stalemate and were tabled. Sayre and Kaufman show the City of New York as a mandarin bureaucracy, dominated by an irresponsible and conservative Board of Estimate. In short, the only dynamic that is consistent through time is that resulting from the continuous efforts of the "nonpolitical" civic bureaucracies to expand. In the process, services are provided within the limits of precedent. A minimal order is maintained. The past is the basis for extrapolation into a future where its rules and rules of thumb may or may not work.

Janowitz has put it succinctly. "Let it be assumed that effective decision-making at the community level is the prerequisite for democratic procedures in the larger political system. Everywhere community leadership faces a common problem, . . . namely, the issue is not the manipulation of the citizenry by a small elite, but rather the inability of elites to create the conditions required for making decisions."[16]

# THE

# PROBLEMS

# OF

# THE

# METROPOLIS

CHAPTER **6**

THE VAST SPRAWL of contiguous and overlapping sites for human activity that makes up a metropolitan complex is fragmented and inchoate in its policy. Disjunction between economic, social, and political boundaries has even led some to dismiss the term "metropolitan community," for existence side by side in space is no guarantee of social structure. Furthermore, the overriding importance of distant organizational centers for such local groups as labor unions, corporations, and branches of state or federal agencies, might lead us to speak more accurately of the large-scale organizational network as the true "community," while the locality is merely a "site." In a mobile and fluid social system, geographical space might well be dropped in favor of social or interactional space.

There is one powerful argument against the strategy. Geographical space is translated into social fact when the locality is a site for social interaction: those who exist side by side share in some respects a common fate. The maintenance of their common scene and its necessary facilities is a requirement for all, for its neglect has repercussions upon the constituent organizations. The various actors share a common fate in the degree to which each is dependent upon some of the neighboring groups, whether as necessary conditions for continued operation or as possible blocks to the ongoing activities of the groups.

The metropolitan complex has housekeeping tasks as old as the history of cities. Failure to accomplish these tasks at the level expected by the corporate citizens is a major source of most "metropolitan problems." The maintenance of public safety and order, of facilities for drainage and water supply and the circulation of people and goods and messages, in our contemporary metropolitan areas, would have been tasks familiar to the city fathers of Memphis and Thebes. In urban communities, contiguity and a resulting interdependence in these matters calls for a coordination of behavior that is not always forthcoming: the results are "problems."

The metropolis as the showcase and treasure house of a society is the center of loot, and its heterogeneous population creates a maximum probability for variation in the norms concerning interpersonal (and interproperty) relations. The prevalence of "strangers" weakens surveillance and encourages individual entrepreneurship, which avoids the market and goes straight to the source of wealth. In the places of public aggregation where the norms are in the keeping of the "police," all cities have been dangerous to a degree. Though we do not need the private army of bodyguards that accompanied Roman Senators on their nighttime jaunts, the citizens of contemporary American metropolitan areas are necessarily cautious at night. And though they are not as ubiquitous as the private wars between private armies in the streets of the Renaissance cities of Italy, the clashing of gangs on the West Side and the pitched battles of mercenaries fighting for company or union would have been familiar enough to Cellini or Aretino. And, just as hardly a day passed in Imperial Rome without several fires (due to faulty heating) and the collapse of a jerry-built tenement, so the contractor and landlord only continue an age-old war with the building inspector in our cities. The yearly holocausts in the tenements of New York, Chicago, and other large cities have long histories and many precedents, as does the collapse of a great bridge or the inundation of a tract-development built on a "dry" river bed on the outskirts of a Texas metropolis. In the great city, milk has often been watered and sugar sanded for "the strangers." All large-scale communities have the problems of order in the organizational interstices, where the tightly interlocked role systems do not function.

Nor is the perennial problem of water supply, waste disposal, and drainage (all interlinked by the tendency of moving water to organize itself in drainage basins coterminous with large settlements) a new one. The major monuments of Rome include the long-distance aqueducts and the fountains for retail distribution. As for waste disposal, the fountains of Rome were frequently used as *pissoirs*, while the burghers of the medieval communes had persistent tendencies to sneak their household garbage onto the public streets at night for others to walk through. And in America today the gentleman, as befits his sex, walks on the outer edge of the sidewalk—for the burghers of London were in the habit of emptying slops directly from their overhanging second stories onto the pedestrian-ways below. These tricks are continued in the suburban municipalities, which empty their communal garbage and sewerage into streams that flow through their neighbors' backyards, and in the paper mill whose effluvia ruin the beaches and creeks of the nearby resort town.

As for transport, the geometry of urban settlement has always created serious problems in the circulatory system. The major innovations of Julius Caesar included an ordinance requiring all goods to be brought into the city at night, for the narrow streets (the Appian Way was less than twenty feet wide) had become so congested with commercial traffic the citizens couldn't get about. As a consequence, the citizens of Rome had to sleep through the neighing of animals, the creak and jar of wooden wheels on cobblestones, and the concomitant cursing of the teamsters.[1]

So much for history. These examples are intended to introduce a perspective from which we may view the metropolitan problem as, in many respects, a predictable outcome of contiguity and function. All of these "problems" are solved more satisfactorily in contemporary American cities than in most cities of the past. Yet the air is filled with talk about "the metropolitan problem." For Americans, so recently denizens of small towns and cities and open-country neighborhoods, are becoming a preponderantly urban nation; the housekeeping problems of cities, and very large cities at that, are well nigh universals. At the same time, the rising level of living brings the citizen to expect more and better governmental services. Seeing the national income soar (and with it his personal income) he is dismayed at the filthy streets of the central city, the rutty lanes of suburbia, the narrow thoroughfares so obviously inadequate for rush-hour traffic, and the waste of industry and the auto that poisons the air he breathes. Discrepancy between the expected and the encountered can be produced by either declining services or ascending expectations.

## Fragmentation of the Urban Polity and Its Causes

As consumption norms for governmental goods rise and the conditions for meeting them grow more complex, there is no accompanying rational development of the normative order and the organizational structure to allow their realization. Many basic goods and services of those who share the common fate of the metropolis are dependent upon coordination of behavior throughout the area—and there is a discrepancy between common fate (and the problems it creates) and a common order for controlling that fate. The metropolitan problems are political problems; they demand binding public decisions on public issues, but the metropolitan complex shares no common government.

The walls between central city and suburbia, and between one suburb and another, are based on the constitutional definition of a community current in an older America. The definitions fit the local communities of rural and small towns; incorporation was easy, annexation or merger difficult, and in time the referendum became the basic method of changing the structure of government. However, the metropolis is not a collection of small towns, villages, and open country lying near a great city. The integration of behavior within an area-wide division of labor and reward, the lay of the drainage basin, the mobility and fluidity of the population from one end of the area to the other —all impose and underline interdependence. Today, the democratic constitutions are used by residential enclaves in the suburbs to guarantee autonomy from the surrounding polity.

In consequence, the powers of the police and the resources of the fisc bear little relationship to the structure of action among the interdependent population.[2] The police power, fragmented among dozens or hundreds of municipalities, is frequently unused and sometimes abused. A suburban force may be quite inadequate at policing a mass strike of the only large industry within municipal limits; its special forte may be, on the other hand, the operating of a "speed trap" that yields revenue for officials and the town. This is facilitated by the common phenomenon of a major route of the journey to work passing through a dozen municipalities, each with a different speed limit, traffic code, and police department.

The fisc is also fractionated and limited as a result of organizational separatism in government. The collection of taxes by whatever municipality happens to have authority frequently means the big taxpayers, the corporate citizens, pay only to one small jurisdiction, while the social costs of their operations may be liabilities in quite different municipalities. The suburban citizen, incorporating his neighborhood and excluding industry, pays dearly for his autonomy. With only a residential tax base, his property taxes shoot upward with the cost of installing a new government and a new physical plant. The effects of fractionalizing the fisc are most dramatically evident in the central city. Still the workshop of the metropolis (a majority of suburbanites work there, including the most highly paid and most powerful), the city government must supply the facilities to get this work done and to transport the suburban army back and forth. The city also houses most of the poor, the unskilled and semiskilled workers who make possible the wealth of suburbia. These burdens require an enormous public expenditure, yet the central city's tax base is static or shrinking.

Most of its industry is "land-locked" while the public facilities that still make it a hub for the region—museums, churches, concert halls, universities, and parks and auditoria—take land off the tax rolls. As the automobile is more widely used the process accelerates, with freeways and interchanges destroying as they create. Thus the central city faces a decline in net worth, while suburban municipalities face continuous fiscal problems due to their citizens' resistance to governmental costs.

The underlying norms of local government in America prescribe local autonomy and direct control by the citizens through referendum elections. Both prescriptions perpetuate existing governments and limit their powers. The direct democracy of the "republic in miniature" operates through a citizenry alienated in the city, ignorant in the suburbs, indifferent in both halves of the metropolis.[3] The resulting incompetence produces a powerful inertia supporting the *status quo*, limiting both the resources and the police power of local government. For the uninvolved citizen tends to believe "that government is best which not only governs least but also *costs least.*"

The very existence of the metropolis is brought about through increase in scale—the extension of the network of interdependence, with a consequent coordination of behavior and resources and with increasing control over the environment. While this occurs, the structure of local government stays constant or shrinks with a multiplication of minute, do-nothing municipalities. The benefits of increasing organizational scale, in coordination, resources, planning, and consequently, control over the environment, are denied the local polity. So constricting has the iron hand of the referendum been, on local government structure, that one suspects none of those great changes in the economy that Americans identify with progress would ever have come about had they been subject to a vote of the citizens.

The organization of the local polity in metropolitan communities has moved in a direction opposite that of other important segments of the society. This has resulted in a violent disjuncture in scale between political organization and the aggregated results of economic organization—that is, between the political city and the socioeconomic city. Wilson and Wilson speak of such disjuncture as the underlying cause of racial conflict in Africa. Nothing so dramatic occurs in the metropolis, but formally the results are similar. Resources are divorced from responsibility; rights are separated from duties.

## Some Results of Smallness of Scale in Local Government

A major result of this lag and lack in local political organization has been discrepancy between the goods and
services produced by government and those produced by
exclusive membership organizations, between the public
and the private sectors of the American economy. The postwar American drives an automobile with fins like a Nike
missile through bumper-to-bumper traffic; lounges by a
private swimming pool that reflects a smoggy sky; carefully threads his way through the city at night, avoiding
not only the slums but the public parks as dangerous and
poorly protected places.

The central city has been deeply affected. It has lived
many years off its earlier investments, exploited by the
population during World War II when building construction and the New Deal had gone to war. With the postwar
boom new investment was channeled to the suburban rings,
not the center. The property has become run down. But
in a rapidly changing society, whose technological revo-
lutions are continually altering the lifeways of the population and the requisite shape of their cities, new investment
and remodeling are repetitive necessities. They do not
come about, automatically, from the play of the market.

If the automobile population of the metropolis is to approximate in numbers the human population, the government (and only the government) can build the requisite
thoroughfares and parking spaces. If citizens take a liking
to home "garbage disposals" the resulting pressure upon
the sewerage system is a problem of the government. If the

metropolis located on a coastal plain with a climatic inversion begins to produce a dense atmosphere of smog correlated with growth and prosperity, the latter are the accomplishments of its private citizens, but the smog is a problem of the government.

A further result of the discrepancy in scale between local government and other aspects of the metropolis is the lack of facilities and powers for over-all planning. The various housekeeping tasks of the city and the new capital investments continually demanded are not isolated enterprises; they are intimately intertwined. As one example, new routes for automobiles will affect and be affected by mass transit, parking facilities, and traffic control systems. New traffic throughways will direct the settlement of new areas and change the land use of old ones. Land use, in turn, defines the need for such services as schools, parks, roads, sewerage, and the like. The building of a circulatory system is, in many respects, a "commitment of the tissues." It traces a structural outline of the city that will emerge. Thus an effort to improve the flow of automobile traffic in a metropolitan area, which seems a simple goal, will inevitably have to take into account the other components of the transport grid—just as it will drastically affect other aspects of the city's collective life. Interdependence among the separate geographical subareas has similar corollaries. Traffic in any one segment of the circulatory system is generated elsewhere; the layout of new residential suburbs decides the traffic pressure on central city arteries, and the decisions of the central city government (as between, say, subsidizing mass transit or building express highways) determine the streets the suburban residents will drive to work. The argument for city planning is the desire to control and foresee the consequences of the necessary house-keeping tasks of the urban populace.

To foresee the results of alternatives, however, requires an organization that has the information. To act with foresight on area-wide problems requires an organization whose sanctions apply across the urban complex as a whole. In the absence of a single polity for the metropolis, growth is uncoordinated and unplanned, with the transport system tending to follow, willy-nilly, the development of new areas controlled by tiny municipalities or not controlled at all, while improved roads precipitate further building and settling. The lack of coordinated policy produces a lack of foresight, perpetuating the tendency to act first and think later that has left the American city continually in arrears on its civic agenda. And, as new development progresses, it represents massive capital investments, not easily to be ignored when future decisions are made. The city of the future loses freedom of choice and becomes a captive of the unplanned commitments of today. Its problems, like those pressing most severely now, will be problems of "redevelopment."

## Ideology and Utopia

Technological change and other aspects of increasing scale have altered the organizational structure of the society, radically transforming the shape of the urban complex. Governmental bounds and powers have not changed accordingly. The results are fatal to any unified policy for the metropolis. The response, among those who consider the metropolis as a problem, has been complex and muddled. Two different images can be perceived, however, in their statements of the problem.

For many, the central business district is the hub and symbolic center of the metropolis—just as the central city is the defining political entity. All else is error, confusion, a result of improper planning in the past. Allowing the unlimited use of the automobile in the city was a mistake, as was unlimited incorporation of suburban municipalities. The solution of the "metropolitan problem" is, in this view, to reconstruct the city of earlier ages—socially and governmentally if not physically. To counteract the automobile, whose use continues the centrifugal movement of population, mass rapid transit must be developed to further funnel the people into the downtown "heart" of the city. To offset fragmentation of government, one big city must be organized, incorporating all the suburbs and the rural-urban fringes that will be the municipalities of tomorrow. Within the new entity, decisions on mass transit, roads and streets, parking, and land use can be coordinated throughout the region; the city can become once more an encompassing community.

Such a community will have a greater public treasury to allocate, and greater powers in its allocation. But it will also be more "responsible," for it will heal the schism in the electorate produced by the "Berlin Wall" of governmental boundaries. Executives, who have given hostages to downtown, will be citizens of the polity that determines the fate of downtown. Negroes and other ethnic groups, excluded from the suburbs by governmental walls, will have more opportunity to move outward as they move upward. The

Democratic Party will have to engage, once more, in competitive politics as Republican voters become part of the larger electorate. Freedom for the future development of the metropolis will be protected through planning for the metropolitan community as a social, economic, and political whole.

These are the ideologists of return.

At the other extreme, however, others recall the words of Patrick Geddes and Lewis Mumford. For them the great city is "megalopolis," an abomination of desolation producing half of what's wrong with the world. Believing that the democratic polity and a healthy society can only be nurtured and maintained in a smaller community, they seek a reintegration of the world of home, work, and the polity, in small satellites without a real sun. They are the utopians of dispersion. Greenbelt communities clustered near one another, integrated through the new technologies of transport and communication, are their ideal communities for the large-scale society. Though organizational transformation of the total society may require giant exclusive membership organizations, it does not require enormous rabbit warrens in place of the local community. In fact, the increasing locational freedom of contemporary man allows him to return to the small-scale local community while retaining the advantages of a new community form, one which reconciles the diverse activities of men in a common scene, while avoiding both the anemic community of limited liability in the suburbs and the massive social dust heap of the central city.

Both ideologists and utopians envisage a kind of policy decision which is not likely to come about in contemporary America.

# Efforts at Metropolitan
# Governmental Reform

In the President's Report on *Recent Social Trends,*
published in 1933, McKenzie spoke of the emergence of a
new social form, the metropolitan region, and with it a
"metropolitan consciousness." [4] He discussed the recent
efforts (as of 1933) to create *metropolitan* governments in
such cities as St. Louis and Pittsburgh. To be sure, the efforts had failed, but he thought the logic of social change
would inevitably produce further efforts. He was correct.
In the intervening twenty-eight years dozens of efforts
have been made to recreate the governmental form of the
city in a metropolitan image; until 1957 there was not one
single success.

And yet the issue has never died. In 1957, in a summary
of activity it was reported that nearly one hundred metropolitan studies and surveys had been conducted in the past
few years.[5] All had been concerned with some or most of
the problems that have been briefly noted; many had
emerged with recommendations for some kind of governmental unification—some integration of social activities over
the fragmented map of the typical metropolis. Both the
record of consistent failure and the continuing efforts at
change are impressive regularities.

A group of "public-minded citizens" formed into a committee typically initiates such action.[6] This group will include crusading metropolitan dailies, aspiring politicians,
and underemployed lawyers. It will be financed by businessmen from the downtown area, utilities, banks, retail
stores, real estate firms—all painfully aware of "the decay of

downtown." It will have enthusiastic cadres among the amateurs of local government, such as the members of the National Municipal League, and the League of Women Voters. Its ideologists will be free-lance public administrators and professors of public administration. They will see clearly, through the results of a survey, how great is the need for a metropolitan government. They will recommend a new charter, whose provisions will range from outright merger of all governments to some form of urban county or federal district, special or general. Finally, since most state constitutions provide fairly accessible machinery, the committee will trip the lever to initiate a referendum for a new charter. Such patterns of action occur repeatedly in many large metropolitan complexes: Cleveland has voted a half-dozen times for some kind of metropolitan government.

The result is failure. Only two metropolitan governments exist in North America. One is in Toronto and was initiated by a Provincial legislature without recourse to the opinions of the Toronto government's electorate. The other is a combination of urban county and federal district plan, which took effect in Dade County, Florida in 1957, and includes Miami and its suburbs in one unit. Though it is too early to measure the results of the one metropolitan government now existing in the United States, the conditions under which it succeeded at the polls are instructive.

Dade County has been one of the fastest growing metropolitan areas in America since the end of World War II, with a great resulting fluidity of community social structure. In 1956 half the population had come in since the end of the war, and this included many of the aspiring leaders. The commitment of people to neighborhood and local area was slight, there was no party apparatus, and thus the influence of neighborhood political leaders was correspondingly weak. The local community press was just beginning to develop a wide coverage while the central city dailies were the dominant media in all parts of the county. Further, local government had suffered from fiscal and statutory incapacities to take care of the population flood that strained all service facilities. Important tasks, such as sewerage disposal, were not dependably performed, while others were simply not performed. As one result, there seems to have been little popular confidence in the central city government: at one time the city of Miami came within a few votes of being legally abolished. Under these circumstances, with the support of nearly all major leaders and with an all-out campaign by the metropolitan daily newspapers, the "Metro" plan won by a few hundred votes.[7]

In short, the typically fragmented organizational structure of the metropolitan area had no chance to get set and the opposition to "Metro" was correspondingly weak. Most areas, however, have developed a complex and cumbersome, but hallowed, organized, and politically effective system. The very fact that it is a system (and one based upon fragmentation) means there will be effective opposition to a governmental revolution. After all, one clue to the existence of a system is its resistance to change and its tendency to return to a steady state. The movements to create new constitutions for the metropolis consistently run head-on into such resistance: defeat of reform probably strengthens the system.

The forces fighting for change have been described. They are an *ad hoc* army, recruited from diverse interests and frequently masking their internal conflicts of interest under the phrase "the metropolitan problem" (for the utopian mode leads us to imagine the radical change will reconcile all such conflicts). The forces fighting against metropolitan government, however, are drawn right out of the roles of government. As working parts of the existing structure they are apt to have political potency as well as governmental positions. Only when there is a split among the incumbents will the forces of change include some of them, but it will usually be a dissident minority tackling the establishment.

In the central city the mayor and his team of incumbents, trusted administrators of a vast governmental machine, images made large by the metropolitan mass media, are the center of opposition. But the "boys in the wards" will also be in opposition; any change in the rules of the game is dangerous to their jobs. (In fact, they will cooperate against party policy and over party lines in mutual protection). The governmental-political cadres will have a widespread influence, especially among the employees of local government (a large army in a metropolitan central city) for even the senior civil servant cannot feel secure when the very entity that employs him, "the city," is in danger of melding into some new, unknown organization. Opposition will be rationalized in many ways: complexes of folk political science will appear as public statements in the newspapers. But major themes, appearing over and over again, are these: fear of the unknown ("big government"), caution ("why rock the boat?" "leave well enough alone"), loyalty to, and pride of place in, the existing city, suspicion that the city will get the short end of the bargain, political suspicion of the crusading outsiders, who are not part of the team and whose campaign comes close to condemnation of the existing government. The normative structure of the existing political and governmental system easily translates the movement for change into a political contest with "the enemy."

In the suburbs the opposition is more diffuse and less professional. But the hundreds of elected suburban officials, the editors of the local community papers, the dozens of municipal attorneys for the suburban towns, the lawyers, real estate brokers, and small businessmen of the outer areas, supply an extremely numerous army of opposition. It is one that is easily organized, for such existing agencies as "leagues of municipalities" and special district governments, law firms and their interconnections, chambers of commerce and Rotary clubs are centers of existing relationships that can become the basis for organized resistance. Opposition will be rationalized in ways quite similar to those of central city opponents. Fear of the unknown, caution, loyalty to a suburban municipality, combine with fear that the city will dominate the new government and thus the suburbs, Democrats lord it over Republicans, while the organized machine of the central city incumbents will find no place for active political suburbanites. In city and suburbs alike the leaders are easily convinced that "the others" will get the better of the bargain.[8]

Such responses will be similar to those of many voters. This is not so much because of the opposition's ability to convince as because of the similarity between the norms of citizen and official with respect to local government. Indeed, fine-spun arguments concerning constitutional powers and the structure of government usually miss the citizen completely, whether voiced by proponents or opponents of the change. Instead, the typical image of the proposed reform is highly simplified. A complex "federal district plan," in which great care is taken to preserve the identity of the suburban municipalities, is as likely as not to be called "merger," by both the citizens who support it and those who oppose it. The niceties of compromise are lost in the vulgarization of the campaign's free market in ideas.

The bifurcation of the metropolitan government between suburbs and central city has created in each a normative structure and a way of defining central city–suburban problems that makes them like the two blades of a scissors. Interacting, they cut proposed governmental reform into a series of paper dolls. Officials in each area see nothing but danger and loss in merger. Citizens look with indifference or anxiety on the prospect. In each case there is a degree of patriotism for the residential area. Central city residents see themselves as inhabitants of a great city and members of a major polity; they have usually been favorable to metropolitan government. Belief in the larger structure has predisposed them "to bring the suburbs back into the city." In recent years, however, there are many signs that they also reject merger; the working class, Negro, and ethnic residents of the central city are not so enthusiastic for a policy of reclaiming the peripheries.[9]

The suburban citizens have never supported merger. They see themselves as residents of a small, local community, made up of friends and neighbors and with "clean government" run by people like themselves. To their separatism, apparently, is now added that of the central city. Each kind of metropolitan separatist has a stake of sorts in his government; to the suburbanite it stands for his neighborhood and way of life, to the central city resident it is a polity within which his class or ethnic enclave has a stake and a voice. Each looks across the "Berlin Wall" at the other, seeing an army of strangers who cannot be trusted with the fate of his treasure.[10]

Behind such definitions may well lie conflicting images of the metropolis as a scene for social life. Those in the city who prefer the complete merger of city and suburbs are disproportionately made up of older persons, born in the city or long resident there, with higher education and more commitment to the city than most. Their patriotism for the city, their desire to see it dominant, may rest upon an ideology of return. But those who prefer some halfway house tend to be younger, suburban, home-owning, and child-rearing. For them a proper image of the metropolis is that of a loose fabric of neighborhoods and local communities, knit together by miles of superhighways, but autonomous in each small residential subarea. Thus feelings of patriotism for the local community, in their case, may rest upon a philosophy or utopia of dispersion, a vulgar form of the small community proposed by Mumford and his sympathizers.[11]

The proponent of such radical change faces a formidable problem. He is disbarred from the organizational networks that support the *status quo*, and he must rely on improvised auditoriums. His message requires considerable education in details—if a person does not see the problems produced by a fractionated polity, the solution will be meaningless to him. Yet such education is a difficult task under any circumstances. When it must rely on a crash campaign in the mass media, the radical message tends to become a simplified nostrum. Its direst possible implications are spelled out (in forms noted earlier) by the legitimate incumbents of local office, who may attract a wide range of respectful attention. And such an ambiguous thing is the hypothetical new charter that it will sustain all manner of innuendo (even outright lying is hard to detect for the citizen who has never read the document).

Of course a great many residents care little for local government anyway. Those who do are usually not educated by such a campaign: they are confused. This confusion is tinctured by anxieties, for the opposition translates in vivid detail the dangers of change. And, being no expert in government, the citizen frequently surrenders—fails to vote at all, or votes against change. Perhaps he invokes the age-old adage of the peasant, "Better the evil that is known...."

And in truth, local government in metropolitan areas is not approaching catastrophe. The government of American cities seems to have improved considerably over the past half century. As the management becomes professionalized and the division of labor clarified, government supplies more and better services, creates a more stable public order, and does so with less corruption and collusion between various private interests and the representatives of the electorate. While the aged and classic building layout of the city has changed rapidly and radically, this has, after all, been in response to the changing demands of the residents. The downtown declines because citizens prefer their suburban shopping centers. The suburbs expand like grass-fire because the urban resident, when he can afford it, prefers to raise his children in the tract developments of the fringe areas, paying taxes to a suburban municipality with a pretty name.

Though the proponents of change frequently resort to crying "wolf!" the metropolis is in no serious danger of disintegration. While there is fairly widespread discontent with some services, there is no groundswell of rebellion at the existing order of government. To be sure, a substantial minority among suburbanites is concerned with the governmental weakness of the new developments, and many people in the central city are anxious that something be done about the ravages of time among the ancient neighborhoods. Throughout the metropolitan areas the regional transportation system is a source of dissatisfaction. But such needs do not justify the dramatic cry of "save our city!" They are, basically, indications of a demand for consumer items in the governmental sector that are in permanent or temporary short supply.[12]

## Functional Equivalents of Metropolitan Government

Freud tells the story of the famous surgeon whose students, during an autopsy, exclaimed over arteries "as thick and hard as ropes"—"No wonder he died!" "But gentlemen," the surgeon remonstrated, "you must remember that he was alive until yesterday." Metropolitan areas, with all their ills, continue to survive and prosper. For one thing, many of their ailments are annoying but not crucial, while for those that might be fatal some expedient solution is eventually devised.

Within the strait jacket of governmental form imposed by the norms of local government and frozen in the state constitutions, a minimal coordination is contrived. The multitudes of small municipalities pool their resources through special districts supplying services ranging from fire protection to schools and parks. These are pieced out by intergovernmental contracts, allowing the criminals of one area to be boarded in the jails of another, or making it possible for several "cities" to share a single water supply. And a certain amount of informal agreement and consultation aids in the disposition of scarce resources and the coordination of policy.[13]

For the area as a whole, important services may be entrusted to a special metropolitan district government. The Chicago and Boston park districts, the Metropolitan St. Louis Sewer District, the Port of New York Authority, are examples of this device. In general, when the politically effective demand for services requiring area-wide development arises and reaches an action point, the typical solution has been such governments. If these precedents are any clue, it is likely that the consumption demands noted earlier will be satisfied, or at least tempered, through such organization and not through the reordering of the metropolitan complex within a single general government.[14]

The fiscal problems of the central city are already being partially solved by the tax on earnings. This simple expedient takes some of the traditional burden off the central city property owner; applying to all who work in the city, it forces the suburban residents who troop in each morning to share the overhead costs of running the city. It is a tax on the *use* of the central city's facilities, not upon residence therein, and it can be voted upon only by the residents of the central city. The logic of such a tax is cognate with a system where home and work are governmentally separated, and it is likely to become a widespread solution.

Another important aid in solving the fiscal problems of the metropolitan area completely by-passes the lack of a local polity. Federal and state subsidy eases the budget crises in central city and suburb alike. In the city the cost of rebuilding thoroughfares of the streetcar age for a population depending on the automobile is greatly accelerated by the Federal Highway Program and such state programs as the California gas-tax program for freeway building. The deteriorated neighborhoods and downtown facilities are renovated through the Federal Urban Renewal Program's Title I. The burdens of caring for the poor are largely carried by outside agencies. The cost of aid to the handicapped, family relief, aid to dependent children, and much of the cost of hospitals and clinics are shared by outside sources. In the suburbs the "new federalism" (as Wood has dubbed it) not only helps with welfare costs, but also subsidizes the tremendous capital expenditures for roads through supporting freeways to the city and circumferential arteries. Any subsidy for public schools is disproportionately useful to suburban areas if it is earmarked for construction. In fact, as state and federal governments support schools and roads in the suburbs, they share the major capital expenditures of the new suburban municipalities.[15]

Such are some of the devices used to circumvent the conservative norms of citizen and politico with respect to local government, and the consequent lack of a contemporary polity for the metropolis. Ironically, powers that are not entrusted to a local government exposed to local voters are handed to federal agencies or to what Bollens has called "the ghost governments" of the special districts. Equally ironic is the curious flow of resources to the area. Bypassing the local fisc (hampered by statutory debt limits, requirements for referenda, and the fragmentation of the tax base) the money is sent to the hub of larger scale government, from which it returns to the metropolitan area. The powers and resources necessary to the urban centers of large-scale society are thus organized *outside* the framework of municipal government, leaving that framework archaic and passive.

The discrepancy in organizational scale between local government and the nature of large-scale society results in a movement of power upward, to organizational centers outside the control of the local polity. Such organizations wield power that is area-wide in scope and consequences. But the use of such power does not require either concern for the interdependence of different aspects of the metropolitan community, or the concern for the ultimate nature of the city that a local polity might implement. In consequence, existing trends are simply accelerated. The rapid development of circumferential highways can only speed up the suburban dispersion. The geometry of the freeways to downtown can only gut the central business district, reducing the symbolic center to an interchange. (Meanwhile, the massive Urban Renewal Program operates at cross-purposes, attempting to lure back the population whose suburban move is facilitated by the Federal Highway Program.) The governmental dichotomy is perpetuated by subsidy of the existing system from both state and federal sources, together with the *pis aller* of special district governments.

Under the circumstances, no agreement is possible on the desirable future shape of the metropolitan community. Common fate is not translated, through communication, into an area-wide normative system, nor could such a system be implemented as a guide to the proper state of things. The only large-scale polity of the metropolis is that of the central city, while the multiplication of suburban municipalities continues at a merry rate. The central city continues to decline and the suburbs continue to boom. The metropolitan area flourishes.

# THE
# CHANGING
# IMAGE
# OF THE
# CITY

CHAPTER **7**

INTELLECTUAL confusion and a problematic empirical ordering seem to be defining traits of the "metropolitan problem." The conceptual framework, already awry through the confusion of ideology, utopianism, and social science is doubly warped by indeterminacy in what we want of the city and the mixed metaphors of our theory. This state of affairs is common in the social sciences today, but it is accentuated by the rate of change in urban society, the unprecedented nature of our present situation, and the pluralistic normative order related to the community.

The contemporary world is one in which the traditional ordering of human behavior through group structures has changed radically. This change has proceeded, not through a weakening of group control, but through a shift in the relative importance of different kinds of group. The changing nature of exclusive membership groups, locality groups, and governmental structures, based upon the underlying transformation in the space-time ratio and the nature of production, present a multitude of facets necessitating study to the student of urban worlds. Some of these have been empirically interrelated through most of the history of urban settlement, but today they are empirically separating, and it is possible for us to make new dissociations —and new conceptual distinctions—that clarify the nature of the problem.

Urbanization has been conventionally used as a summary term for three different processes: (1) the growth of cities, (2) the increase in scale of a society, and (3) the culture of city dwellers, or urbanism. In the past the physical existence of the urban concentration was the most dramatic evidence of increase in scale, and was sometimes identified with it. (Thus Durkheim attempts to derive the division of labor from congestion.) In the same way, so isolated was the city from its hinterland that the "urban" life style was as distinctive as an ethnic variation. "Civilization" has its roots, as word and fact, in the enclave of traders, artisans, and rulers who existed within a sea of rustics.

It is clear today that increase in societal scale is the key process. The organizational transformation of the society, which binds in large networks of interdependence a region or a nation, makes possible and requires those concentrations of control centers and population we call cities.

But at the same time, changes in the social organization resting upon interdependence result in drastic modifications of the urban settlement and its relation to the total society. The sheer size of the metropolitan population is impressive. More impressive are two trends: (1) increasing dispersion of population in space, and (2) increasing dispersion of the control centers formulating the dominant decisions that affect its order and shape.

The third process is also affected by increase in scale. There is in America today a consistent decline in the differentiation and social distance between countryman and urbanite. This rests also upon technological changes that have allowed a mastery of space never known before—one that makes possible rapid and precise communication and coordination of behavior across great differences. The culture of the large-scale society is urban in its essence; all ears are tuned to the nationwide communication networks, and behavior is ordered by the large-scale agencies of governmental bureau, corporation, and national market. In brief, the organizational necessities that once produced spatial density and a high degree of local autonomy are no longer coercive. The independent factory becomes the branch plant, while the nation-wide governmental agency pre-empts tasks once locally performed. Organizational space is a function of the shrinking space-time ratio.

It is clear that increase in scale is apt to continue. The web of interdependence continues to grow, with increasing specialization and differentiation of behavior and with increasingly complex mechanisms for integrating this behavior. The use of two-way telecommunication, supersonic aircraft, digital computers, and other innovations in communication and control make possible ever further increase in scale—and further conquest of geographical space. The growth and structure of cities becomes a dependent variable. Rather than the generator and limiting condition of increasing scale, the city is simply the convenient spatial location for centers of control, work, and residence. And convenience shifts with the demands of the national system. Thus the study of the city is the study of one temporary product of increasing scale—the changing nature of the human settlement.

## Organizational Analysis of the City

Considering the city as the dominant human community at this point in the history of the society of increasing scale, the relevant strategy is one that emphasizes the organizational structure and its dynamics. Such analysis subsumes *relevant* portions of political, economic, and conventional sociological analysis. But they become relevant *only* if they contribute to the organizational image of the city.

Thus, the approach is similar to that predicted by Reiss—the study of community, but it is a concept of community that requires a concentration upon the organizational demands of locality groups made up of exclusive membership groups in interaction. It leads to a concern with the structure of norms, with the flow of communication that diffuses them, and with the sanctions that produce predictable behavior and effective coordination. In studying each of these three aspects of community organization, it is necessary to draw upon analyses of such problem areas as industrial organization, ethnic and social class distinctions, and mass communications. These subjects are requisite to that study insofar as their findings are relevant to organizational analysis. The organizational dynamics of the society, working through the economic and political segments, continually create social differentiation that is culturally consolidated and becomes in turn the basis for further organizational evolution. Social differentiation and suborganization lead to problem fields and specialties in social science, but the latter can always be translated back to its origin through the vocabulary of concepts.

An organizational image of the city requires information about types of interdependence, communication flow, norms and sanctions—in short, the ongoing, everyday activities of the constituent groups that create a complex and relatively stable social structure among the mass of human individuals in space. Such structures have constraining power over individuals; thus they allow the social scientist predictive power. We must emphasize the description of households, neighborhoods, local residential communities, municipalities, and metropolitan political arenas, both in abstraction and in complex interaction. At the level of the individual actor, we concentrate upon his path through a social maze. Social science is not concerned with the internal psychological field of the actor, but it is obsessed with the architecture of the maze, and the study of a random sample of urbanites may be an effective tracer of a society's organizational structure.

The massive changes at the societal level must be related through specific arguments to the everyday behavior of men if we are to study the urban community. The interrelations among industrialization, bureacratization, and the growth of cities, at the societal level alone, tell us little about the organizational structure in which concrete (and observable) individuals act and interact. The bureaucratic world of the "organization man" is not translated directly into a bureaucratic local community; quite the contrary—the suburban residences of these company men are a curious reversal in the trend toward increasing scale. The magnates of international corporations are citizens of tiny municipalities with minuscule politics. To study organizational structure we must place it in its relevant scene. That congeries of contiguous and overlapping sites called the metropolitan area is, today, a most relevant scene.

## The City and the Metropolitan Region

The image of the city as a sovereign state, a military power, an integrated and powerful governmental unit, has eroded with the increasing scale of the carrying society. But what remains is not a vacuum to be neglected in our concern with the nation-state. It is a vast interconnected system of organizations operating in an inherited physical landscape and sharing in many respects a common fate. The metropolitan region is the local community of contemporary man. Though he uses it selectively, with an axis that runs from Westchester County to Madison Avenue (or from Cicero to the Black Belt) his selective use merely indicates the enormous complexity of the system —the differentiation of life patterns and the machinery of integration which keeps this human landscape stable and viable for his own path through social space.

Those who cry "Danger!" at the disjunction between the official polity of the metropolis and its burgeoning problems of growth, planning, equity, and service have perhaps retained too great a loyalty to earlier images of the city. Emphasizing the lack of central authority, they have obscured the degree of order that prevails.[1] The metropolis, after all, is in no danger from invasion or collapse; it is supported by a national system. It works within broad tolerance limits and within these limits a minimal order maintains. When "problems" are potentially lethal, the machinery for problem solving begins its creaky action —developing *ad hoc* solutions, expedients, special districts, or federal intervention. The metropolitan community is continuously improvised; its evolution is organic, not rational; change is crescive, not revolutionary; problems are solved by trial and error, not by fiat.

The specialized tasks within the metropolis change location as a result of changing modes of integration. As transport makes possible greater locational freedom, the older central city becomes a specialized area in which the newer migrants are acculturated, the poor are cared for, the working class has a home. Abandonment of the older residential neighborhoods by suburb-bound whites provides improved housing for the segregated ethnics. The changing complexion of the central city electorates gives the "insulted and injured" a greater say in the polity here than anywhere else in America.[2] And within the working-class city the public monuments still stand symbolizing the center of the region. More important, as a result of urban geometry, within the central city lies the interchange of the area-wide transportation grid, the center of area-wide activities, and most of the great industrial concentrations. There is little danger that the central city will become a ghost town.

Nor is there much danger of its attracting its old-style residents back from the suburbs. The suburban areas will be the center of gravity for the masses of the metropolitan population for some time to come. Their choice of life style and their resulting household needs send them inevitably to the ranch houses on the peripheries. Here they develop the suburban neighborhoods and the communities of limited liability. Their differentiated portion of the metropolitan community remains an integral part of the whole, dependent upon the transportation grid and the interchange for its existence.

The over-all polity is, however, a sum of efforts ranging from those of neighborhood improvement associations to the negotiations between central city mayor and the plenipotentiaries of powerful organizations. In the absence of a central arena and polity, the public decisions are made in response to the politically potent demands of a fragmented electorate and the professional concerns of the political managerial elite. They suffice to accomplish a minimal ordering.[3] Freeways are extended rapidly from each part of the periphery to the central interchange and the circumferential patterns multiply. The dozens of municipalities in the suburbs form a League of Municipalities and hire a professional manager; an organizational system is evolved which handles, adequately, some of the problems produced by contiguity and a common fate.

Such developments further reinforce the geographically defined dichotomy of the metropolis, solving the problems created by governmental split in the interdependent population. The resulting unit resembles, in its complexity and lack of symmetry, the government of a total large-scale society. The social scientist is dismayed and a little embittered by the lack of fit between the existing system and any simple, powerful, and elegant theory—much less his notion of a proper city government. His theoretical and normative yearning probably leads him to accentuate the deviation of the metropolis from such order. When, however, he continues empirical investigation of the polity, whether at the township, city, metropolitan, state, or federal level, he is forced to acknowledge again and again the looseness of the system through which our political fate is evolved.

Such may be the inseparable conditions of public decision-making in a society of increasing scale. The metropolitan community is without a moral and legal father, without a stable hierarchy, without obedient estates, without simple policy questions of right *or* wrong. It is, in this sense, the large-scale society in miniature.

## The Future of the City

As the organizational transformation of the society continues, new sources of energy allow further decentralization of work, new techniques of communication and transport allow further spread of organization. In the hinterland of any contemporary metropolis one encounters the industrial parks and planned residential developments that signify freedom from the locational determinants of other days. Still further away, along a "country" highway far from any major city, one may see continuous development spreading for twenty or thirty miles—roadtowns, for which the highway is Main Street.

The decentralization of residence, work, and play,

around the metropolitan area, along with governmental fragmentation, are perhaps mere beginnings. Other functions, once considered native and proper only to the central city, may as easily be decentralized. Universities are experimenting with branch campuses and state-wide educational systems; there is no discernible reason that such cultural manifestations as ballet, symphony, and theatre should not rotate their performances through the giant subcenters that spring up where the freeways cross the circumferential highways. Perhaps only a lingering Puritanism persuades us that the person who is unwilling to devote two hours to transportation to and from the central business district has no right to "culture." The burgeoning little theatres and galleries throughout the Los Angeles metropolitan area may be some indication that the cultural dominance of the central business district is near an end. The patrons and customers of the arts are in the suburbs, notwithstanding the tropism of their creators for the center. Furthermore a great locational decentralization of entertainment has already taken place, through television, radio, and the movies. The locational requirements for a flourishing "high culture" are now, to say the least, highly problematic, but the odds on maintaining the Downtown simply as a home for such performances would seem low.

Meanwhile, with the limited number of future migrants from the backwoods to the central city and the increasing spread of residences possible on the peripheries, it seems likely that the city will lose its monopoly of residential areas for colored persons. Though many may still choose the central city as a local area, many others only await the freedom from income and ethnic restrictions to move to newer and more convenient sites outside the congested center. As this occurs, the central city will require either an immensely expensive rebuilding or an orderly liquidation.

Whether the city can be rebuilt as a residential site is very problematical. For those who see the central city as "hallowed ground," no effort could be too great, and the polity as an economic force does not follow the rules of the market. It is possible that the ideologists of return, who envisage a central city organized in super-blocks and including headquarters, offices, apartments for those urbane in their life style, bohemias, public monuments, parks, and a limited number of single-family residences, will eventually prevail. Certainly the locational advantages of the central city can be greatly enhanced by developmental funds from the public treasury—and one could undoubtedly bribe middle-class persons to live in the center under some circumstances. However, without such efforts it seems doubtful that the locational demand of either industry or residential households will justify the enormous expense of razing much of the present structure and rebuilding. Thus a gradual shrinkage in the use-value of the central city as a whole seems inevitable in the short run.

Anthony Downs, a location economist, has indicated some preconditions for a "recentralized city." [4] They are basic and major governmental programs that, in turn, will prime the pump for the use of private capital. They include clearance of many obsolete structures throughout the gray areas; a rigorous enforcement of housing and building codes to make owning slum property unprofitable; a massive improvement in policing to guarantee safety of person and property throughout the central city neighborhoods; the redevelopment of residential areas in very large blocks (at least as large as high school districts); redevelopment in *homogeneous* blocks that, similar in life style and social rank, would be competitive with suburban areas; maintenance and development of metropolis-wide cultural facilities in the central cities; and the creation of a transport grid that is meant to encourage and serve high-density residential areas.

Such a program would, in effect, suburbanize the central city's declining neighborhoods. It would require, however, very consistent and radical action by government—and we must recall the fragmented and immobilized state of local government in the metropolis. We must also remember Wood's remarks: New York City's redevelopment program, the largest and most vigorous in the nation, has completed, planned, or in progress, the renovation of one thousand acres.[5] Five thousand acres need such renovation, and, so rapidly do neighborhoods change, the figure of five thousand acres may remain undiminished by the time present work is complete. One reason for the paucity of the response to blight is the enormously expensive practice of "writing off" or subsidizing the difference between present market value and value as new land. (Vernon's estimate of the cost is approximately $160,000,-000 per square mile of cleared land.)[6] As Downs argues, this would be much lower if the *legal* uses and restrictions of slum dwellings were regulated by government. But what central city political regime, dependent on the support of Negroes and the poor, has the determination to condemn thousands of dwellings and thus evict large and visible symbols of their supporting electorate? Central city governments are, in their way, as poor in political resources as the fragments of suburbia.

What is more likely, in the foreseeable future, is a continued dispersion of human activities and their sites within the metropolitan regions. Further, in a society of increasing scale in which wealth of all types multiplies, we may expect to see an increasing dispersion of metropolitan areas over the nation. And here it is worth remembering that such new areas have advantages over older ones comparable to those of suburbs over central cities: it is cheaper to build new plants from scratch if locational needs are comparable.[7] In the larger system, moreover, many functions can easily be allocated best in terms of such resources as climate—others can be practically location free. Such cities are typically continental assets, with a continental market—not mere centers for their hinterland and region. (Miami and Las Vegas, for example, are clearly without visible means of local support.) Los Angeles has grown from the beginning as part of the national market, for its hinterland includes chiefly desert and national parks. Phoenix, San Diego, Albuquerque, cities of phenomenal recent growth, continue the trend. The spread of metropolitan areas and the spread within each of them point to the possibility of loosely related complexes spreading over enormous distances—*regional cities*. In such cities no local subarea would have the density common to Chicago, Philadelphia, or New York, yet all would be easily accessible to other subareas through rapid transport and instantaneous communication.

Extrapolating from current trends, and utilizing Vernon's work on the New York Metropolitan Area, Downs sees the alternative to a recentralization of the city in these terms.[8] "By the year 2000 the nation will find itself with several large 'conurbations' of solid settlement, such as the Eastern Seaboard from Boston to Norfolk and west to Philadelphia, the West Coast from Santa Barbara south to Tiajuana and from Santa Rosa south to San Jose and west to Sacramento, and a vast weblike network in the Midwest uniting St. Louis, Chicago, Cleveland, Detroit, Indianapolis, Buffalo, and other cities along major freeways and railroads. According to this extrapolation model of future cities, more than 100 per cent of all metropolitan population growth will occur in suburbs, since central cities will actually lose population."

Should this occur, the structure of the city as we know it would be at an end. The process of increase in scale, nurtured in cities and once thought of as unique to them, will have so transformed the society as to eliminate any need for urban centers. Such a society might be larger in scale than any we can conceive today, and its ways of life might well be described as "urbane" if not urban, but settlement would be freed from spatial limitations, and the city would be no more.

Our options are not great. As C. Wright Mills has noted, there seems to be an "organizational demiurge" central to contemporary social change.[9] As it leads to efforts at predictability by the actors in one organization, these efforts tend to result in merger, accomodation, the rationalizing of the organizational environment. Thus, the networks of interdependence in the society continually expand, and from interdependence evolves an increasingly large organizational system. The more complex and mutually contingent the resulting social structure, the fewer its alternative courses of development. The way back to a simpler, smaller-scale society, is barred in the near future at least by the commitments necessary to insure the survival of the one that exists: only catastrophe can radically transform the evolution.

As organizational systems grow in scale the sacred values and esthetic themes of urban man are also changing. Today the ethos of an older city life leads us to feel the shock of disorientation when we consider that the central areas of St. Louis, Chicago, or Cleveland will never again be the symbol and hub of the entire urban community. Watching the decline of central city neighborhoods it is hard to resist a pious nostalgia and regret—and the suburban villas are no substitute for the communal life that is crumbling. Much of the culture, folklore, and ways of life that once stood for the city are casualties of change, for organizational transformation, like Shiva, destroys as it creates.

Among the casualties may also be the concept of local government as a democratic polity. We have noted that the small-scale nature of municipal government leads to its acquiescence in decisions made by large-scale organizations—corporations, unions, the federal government, the Port Authority, or the semiorganized markets. Such acquiescence means that significance evaporates: the local polity is largely irrelevant to the over-all position of the citizens. This, in turn, weakens the competence of local bodies. The entire process may be, however, circumscribed by one phrase—the increase in societal scale. Recalling the discussion of scale above, two aspects are crucial: it increases dependence upon large organization and distant centers of control specific to a limited membership—and it decreases dependence upon the near at hand, the locality group.

Thus it strikes at the roots of the polity as a significant arena for the individual.

Indeed, it is likely that increase in scale is eventually inimical to the democratic local polity. Kitto's analysis of the decline and degradation of the Athenian polity rests, finally, upon the "turning away of the citizens" from community affairs. Such withdrawal is common to both the Republican politics of the Midwestern country towns and the "power elite" in large cities. It reflects the movement of significance, which follows organization, away from the locality group. Whether, and how, it might be recaptured is a subject for speculation—but not in this book.[10]

So the older city appears to be dying—functionally, structurally, politically, and eventually, ideologically. Yet the compliance of the population with these changes we have noted has hardly been forced—indeed, as Wood points out, policy seems to follow the market. And, for the average man, the contemporary metropolis is a vast improvement over his share of the older city. Out of the row houses and tenements, the streetcar and the loft building, he has moved to the ranch house with its patio and two-car garage, the job in the pastel industrial park, the television, the children. . . .

# NOTES

## Chapter 1

1. Philip M. Hauser, *Population Perspectives*, New Brunswick, N.J.: Rutgers University Press, 1960, "The Metropolitan Area Explosion: The Facts," Chapter 4, page 101.

2. *Ibid.*, pp. 101-106.

3. Don Martindale, "Prefatory Remarks: The Theory of the City," in Max Weber, *The City* (translated by Don Martindale and Gertrud Neuwirth), New York: The Free Press of Glencoe, 1958, p. 62.

4. Albert J. Reiss, Jr., in "Introduction: The Sociology of Urban Life, 1946–1956," in Paul K. Hatt and Albert J. Reiss, Jr. (eds.), *Cities and Society, The Revised Reader in Urban Sociology*, New York: The Free Press of Glencoe, 1957, pp. 10-11.

5. "Urban Production and Distribution," in "The Metropolis in Ferment," *Annals of the American Academy of Political and Social Science*, 314, 20-21. Donald M. Pappenfort has made a similar observation: from a conventional ecological point of view the metropolis is not a discrete entity at all, in his opinion. See "The Ecological Field and the Metropolitan Community: Manufacturing and Management," *American Journal of Sociology*, 69, 380-385.

6. For typical works see José Ortega y Gasset, *The State of the Masses;* Oswald Spengler, *Decline of the West;* Emile Durkheim, *The Division of Labor in Society* (translated by George Simpson), New York: The Free Press of Glencoe, 1949 (especially the Preface to the Second Edition); Ferdinand Tonnies, *Gemeinschaft und Gesellschaft* (translated by Charles P. Loomis as *Community and Society*), East Lansing, Mich.: Michigan State University Press, 1957.

7. For extensive and lively documentation of this melodramatic definition, see Anselm Strauss, *Images of the American City*, New York: The Free Press of Glencoe, 1961, particularly Chapter 10, "Rural Aspects of Metropolitan Living." Closer to home is his "Appendix: A Note on Imagery in Urban Sociology."

8. For examples of this approach see Mable A. Elliott and Francis E. Merrill, *Social Disorganization*, New York: Harper and Brothers, 1941; and Robert E. L. Faris, *Social Disorganization*, New York: The Ronald Press, 1948.

9. Harvey W. Zorbaugh, *The Gold Coast and the Slum*, Chicago: University of Chicago Press, 1929; E. Franklin Frazier, *The Negro Family in Chicago*, Chicago: University of Chicago Press, 1932; Nels Anderson, *The Hobo*, Chicago: University of Chicago Press, 1923.

10. Louis Wirth, "Urbanism as a Way of Life," *American Journal of Sociology*, 44, 1-24. For a later statement more directly addressed to the mass-society hypothesis see his article on "Consensus and Mass Communications" in the *American Sociological Review*, 13, 1-15.

11. Emil Lederer, *State of the Masses.*

12. David Riesman, with Reuel Denny and Nathan Glazer, *The Lonely Crowd*, New Haven: Yale University Press, 1950; William H. Whyte, Jr., *The Organization Man*, New York: Simon and Schuster, 1956; Samuel Lubell, *The Future of American Politics*, Garden City, N. Y.: Doubleday and Company, Inc. (Anchor Edition), 1956 and *The Revolt of the Moderates*, New York: Harper and Brothers, 1956; A. C. Spectorsky, *The Exurbanites*, Philadelphia: J. B. Lippincott Company, 1955; John R. Seeley, R. Alexander Sim, and Elizabeth W. Loosly, *Crestwood Heights*, *A Study of the Culture of Suburban Life*, New York: Basic Books, Inc., 1955.

## *Chapter 2*

1. In R. D. McKenzie's classic statement, "The Rise of Metropolitan Communities," *Recent Social Trends in the United States*, Report of the President's Research Committee on Social Trends, New York: The McGraw-Hill Book Co., Inc., 1933.

2. These three dimensions were first identified by Eshref Shevky and Marilyn Williams in *The Social Areas of Los Angeles*, Berkeley and Los Angeles: University of California Press, 1949; the theory upon which they depend is further explicated in *Social Area Analysis* by Eshref Shevky and Wendell Bell, Stanford: Stanford University Press, 1955.

3. This concept in the form used here is first discussed fully by Godfrey and Monica Wilson in *The Analysis of Social Change*, London: Cambridge University Press, 1945. Shevky and Bell discuss it in relation to urbanization (Shevky and Bell, *op. cit.*).

4. The phrase is McKenzie's (see "The Rise of Metropolitan Communities," *op. cit.*).

5. Colin Clark has noted the increasing importance of service and control occupations as a basic characteristic of urban economies. The detailed reasons are discussed by Florence in the analysis of what he calls "economic government."

Both treatments are congruent with Pirenne's discussion of the city's *raison d'être* (Colin Clark, *The Conditions of Economic Progress*, London: Macmillan and Company, Ltd., 1951, 2nd ed.; P. Sargent Florence, *The Logic of British and American Industry: A Realistic Analysis of Economic Structure and Government*, London: Routledge and Kegan Paul, Ltd., 1953; Henri Pirenne, *Medieval Cities: Their Origins and the Revival of Trade*, Princeton: Princeton University Press, 1925).

6. The basic importance of transport was pointed out by Charles Horton Cooley in his doctoral dissertation; a recent discussion of the effects of transport changes on location and use is that of Gilmore. A shrewd discussion of transport, land use, and suburbanization is found in a recent article by Schnore (Charles Horton Cooley, "The Theory of Transportation," in *Sociological Theory and Social Research*, R. C. Angell (ed.), New York: Holt, Rinehart, and Winston, 1930; Harlan W. Gilmore, *Transportation and the Growth of Cities*, New York: The Free Press of Glencoe, 1953; Leo Schnore, "The Growth of Metropolitan Suburbs," *American Sociological Review*, 22, 165-172). Useful also is William F. Ogburn's discussion of "Inventions of Local Transportation and the Patterns of Cities" (reprinted in Hatt and Reiss, *Cities and Society, op. cit.*).

7. A wide range of studies support this view. Best known and (in respect to the relations among occupation, residence, and social honor) still most central are the works of W. Lloyd Warner and his students. (See the "Yankee City Series," Yale University Press.) A recent and stimulating analysis of the social meaning of the residential address is that of James Beshers in *Urban Social Structure*, New York: The Free Press of Glencoe, 1962.

8. For an elaboration of this approach see Scott Greer, *Social Organization*, New York: Random House, 1955.

9. It will be noted that the term "social process" is used in a somewhat unconventional fashion. In this approach, a key difference in the basis for interdependence is that between *social product* (that which has exchange value) and *social*

*process,* or interaction as a value and end in itself. This distinction is based upon the analyses of Robert M. MacIver and Charles H. Page in *Society: An Introductory Analysis,* New York: Holt, Rinehart, and Winston, Inc., 1949. It is further developed in Greer, *Social Organization, op. cit.* The phrase "the social surplus," is from George C. Homans, *The Human Group,* New York: Harcourt, Brace and Company, 1950.

10. The utility and limits of the ecological metaphor are apparent in Norton Long's treatment of "The Metropolitan Community as an Ecology of Games," *American Journal of Sociology,* 64, 251-261.

11. The consequences of a shifting space-time ratio for societies and cities are discussed at considerable length in "Traffic, Transportation, and the Problems of the Metropolis," Scott Greer, in *Contemporary Social Problems,* Robert K. Merton and Robert A. Nisbet (eds.), New York: Harcourt, Brace and Company, 1961. For a careful analysis of societal consequences, see George R. Taylor, *The Transportation Revolution: 1815–1860,* in the "Rinehart Economic History of America Series," New York: Holt, Rinehart, and Winston, 1951.

12. The shifts in occupational distribution are spelled out in Colin Clark, *op. cit.* Florence, *op. cit.,* shows in detail the causes and consequences of increasing scale of economic enterprise, and its effects upon occupational distribution. For a general discussion of societies as energy-transformation systems see Fred Cottrell's brilliant study, *Energy and Society,* New York: The McGraw-Hill Book Co., Inc., 1955. The argument of this chapter relies heavily upon his analyses, as well as those previously cited by Wilson and Wilson and by Shevky and Bell.

13. Henri Pirenne, *The History of Europe,* New York: Doubleday Co. (Anchor Edition), 1959. Shevky and Bell, *op. cit.,* p. 10. For an excellent study relating function to urban settlement see Jack P. Gibbs and Walter T. Martin, "Urbanization and Natural Resources: A Study in Organizational Ecology," *American Sociological Review,* 23, p. 140.

For a recent work on the relationship between function and location of metropolitan complexes in the United States see *Metropolis and Region* by Otis Dudley Duncan, W. Richard Scott, Stanley Lieberson, Beverly D. Duncan, and Hal H. Winsborough, Baltimore: Johns Hopkins Press, 1960.

14. See, for example, Ralph Turner, *The Great Cultural Traditions*, New York: The McGraw-Hill Book Co., Inc., 1941, especially Chapter XX, Vol. 2, "Structure and Process in Cultural Development." Gilmore also has some useful observations on the relationships between organization and transport, *Transportation and the Growth of Cities, op. cit.*

15. Hughes has presented a case study of the conflict of norms between small-scale agrarian society and large-scale corporate enterprise, in *French Canada in Transition*, Chicago: University of Chicago Press, 1943. The conflict arising when norms based upon family and ethnic identity confront norms of bureaucracy (and some rationalizations arising therefrom) is analyzed in "Queries Concerning Industry and Society Growing Out of the Study of Ethnic Relations and Industry," *American Sociological Review*, 14, 211-220.

16. Arthur J. Vidich and Joe Bensman have recently documented these consequences for a small town in New York State in *Small Town in Mass Society*, Princeton: Princeton University Press, 1959. They emphasize both the consequences of disappearing autonomy and the ideological responses to them. Nisbet has treated the matter with an emphasis upon the usurpation of local autonomy by arms of the nation state, in *The Quest for Community: A Study in the Ethics of Order and Freedom*, New York: Oxford University Press, 1953, especially Part Two, "The State and Community."

17. Rudolph Heberle in "Observations on the Sociology of Social Movements," *American Sociological Review*, 14, 354-355, has made the observation that much of the sectionalism of American society, its variation in culture by region, is in some degree an optical illusion, for the changing configuration of economic enterprise is the key variable between regions. As it shifts and is integrated in larger networks of

control, regionalism gives way to national categories. Samuel Lubell has applied the same distinction between region and class in his *Future of American Politics, op. cit.* He predicts the emergence of truly national parties, based on nation-wide class interviews, in his final chapter, "The Nation State."

18. Arthur Ross has discussed the common framework of discourse between union and management representatives implied in collective bargaining situations in *Trade Union Determinants of Industrial Wage Policy*, Berkeley and Los Angeles: University of California Press, 1949. The translation of interorganizational relationships into role requirements of leaders is explored in *Last Man In: Racial Access to Union Power*, by Scott Greer, New York: The Free Press of Glencoe, 1959.

## Chapter 3

1. For a recent study based upon some current notions of situs, see Richard T. Morris and Raymond J. Murphy, "The Situs Dimension in Occupational Structure," *American Sociological Review*, 23, 231.

2. Readership of the "women's magazines" was closely related to a familistic way of life, attendance at movies to a more urban style, in several Los Angeles areas studied (Scott Greer and Ella Kube, *Urban Worlds: A Comparative Study of Four Los Angeles Areas*, Los Angeles: Laboratory in Urban Culture, Occidental College, 1955). David Riesman has recorded his impression of the wide variability in life style, both in work and at play (*The Lonely Crowd, op. cit.,* especially "Glamorizers, Featherbedders, Indispensables," pp. 302-337, and "The Forms of Competence," pp. 330-338).

3. Some of the persisting political effects of ethnicity are documented in "Catholic Voters and the Democratic Party: Persistence and Change in a Historic Relationship," by Scott Greer, *Public Opinion Quarterly*, Winter, 1961.

4. There have been a number of studies indicating the independence and importance of the life-style dimension for

social behavior. Some examples are, "Urban Neighborhood Types and Participation in Formal Organizations," Wendell Bell and Maryanne T. Force, *American Sociological Review*, 21, 23-33; Wendell Bell and Marion T. Boat, "Urban Neighborhoods and Informal Social Relations," *American Journal of Sociology*, 62, 391-398; Wendell Bell, "Anomie, Social Isolation and the Class Structure," *Sociometry*, 20, 105-116; Scott Greer and Ella Kube, *Urban Worlds, op. cit.*; Scott Greer, "Urbanism Reconsidered: A Comparative Study of Local Areas in the Metropolis," *American Sociological Review*, 21, 19-24; Scott Greer and Ella Kube, "Urbanism and Social Structure: A Los Angeles Study," in Marvin Sussman (ed.), *Community Structure and Analysis*, New York: Thomas Y. Crowell Co., 1959; "Voting in a Metropolitan Community: An Application of Social Area Analysis," Walter C. Kaufman and Scott Greer, *Social Forces*, "The Social Structure and Political Process of Suburbia: An Empirical Test," Scott Greer, *Rural Sociology* (in press). A strong case for the emergence of familistic neighborhoods in suburbia was made by E. Gartley Jaco and Ivan Belknap, in "Is a New Family Form Emerging in the Urban Fringe?," *American Sociological Review*, 18, 551-557. For another kind of empirical argument placing life style above income as a basis for residential concentration, see Arnold S. Feldman and Charles Tilly, "The Interaction of Social and Physical Space," *American Sociological Review*, 25, 877-883.

5. Fred Cottrell, *Energy and Society, op. cit.*, especially Chapter 5. For a description and explanation of the paleotechnic city see Lewis Mumford, *Technics and Civilization*, New York: Harcourt, Brace, 1934.

6. Cf. Schnore, *op. cit.* As Schnore implies, the familistic households might accept quarters in the older central city if such quarters could be made comparable to the suburban tract-houses. The point is moot until very large-scale rebuilding occurs in the center—an unlikely development in his view.

7. For the appropriate sources, see Note 6 to Chapter 1.

8. Wirth, "Urbanism as a Way of Life," *op. cit.*; Georg

Simmel, "The Metropolis and Mental Life," in Kurt H. Wolff (trans.), *The Sociology of Georg Simmel*, New York: The Free Press of Glencoe, 1950.

9. R. M. MacIver, *The Web of Government*, New York: Holt, Rinehart, and Winston, Inc., 1947.

10. Mirra Komarovsky, "The Voluntary Associations of Urban Dwellers," *American Sociological Review*, 11, 686-698; Morris Janowitz, *The Community Press in an Urban Setting*, New York: The Free Press of Glencoe, 1952; Donald L. Foley, *Neighbors or Urbanites? A Study of a Rochester District*, The University of Rochester Studies of Metropolitan Rochester, Rochester, New York: 1952; Sylvia Fleis Fava, "Suburbanism as a Way of Life," *American Sociological Review*, 21, 34-37; Morris Axelrod, "Urban Structure and Social Participation," *American Sociological Review*, 21, 13-18; Bell and Force, *op. cit.*; Bell and Boat, *op. cit.*; Greer and Kube, *op. cit.*; Greer, "Urbanism Reconsidered: A Comparative Study of Local Areas in the Metropolis," *op. cit.*; Greer, "The Social Structure and Political Process of Suburbia: An Empirical Test," *op. cit.* For a summary of older studies and studies in smaller cities, see "Membership and Participation in Voluntary Organizations," J. C. Scott, Jr., *American Sociological Review*, 33, 315-326. For a summary of results obtained from national samples, see C. R. Wright and H. H. Hyman, "Voluntary Association Membership of American Adults; Evidence from National Sample Surveys," *American Sociological Review*, 23, 284-294.

11. Ernest W. Burgess and Harvey J. Locke, *The Family: From Institution to Companionship*, New York: American Book Company, 1954 (2nd ed.).

12. O. A. Oeser and S. B. Hammond (eds.), *Social Structure and Personality in a City*, New York: The Macmillan Company, 1954.

13. Greer and Kube, *op. cit.*

14. Elton Mayo, *The Social Problems of an Industrial Civilization*, Boston: Harvard University Graduate School of Business Administration, 1945.

15. Wilbert E. Moore, *Industrial Relations and the Social Order*, New York: The Macmillan Company, 1945. For a succinct statement by Moore see "Industrial Sociology: Status and Prospects," *American Sociological Review*, 13, 382-390, especially "The Industrial Worker and His Environment." Oeser and Hammond, *op. cit.*, make some cognate generalizations with respect to labor in Australia.

16. Will Herberg, "Bureaucracy and Democracy in Trade Unions," *Antioch Review*, 2, 405-417.

17. For an analysis of unions with respect to participation and representation, see Greer, *Last Man In, op. cit.*

18. Riesman, *et al., op. cit.*

## Chapter 4

1. Shevky and Bell, *op. cit.*, pp. 14-15.

2. "Residential Mobility, 1949-1950, in the Ten Largest Standard Metropolitan Areas in the United States," Detroit Area Study, Survey Research Center, University of Michigan, Project 843, No. 1211, May, 1957.

3. For example: "To make generalizations about a modern city in terms of night-time statistics is to provide wrong answers to questions nobody wants answered. What people do at night when asleep throws little light upon the more important daylight activities of urbanites." (E. Gordon Ericksen, review of Shevky and Williams, *The Social Areas of Los Angeles, op. cit.*) The concept of a residential area as only a kind of shelf upon which the dormant body is stored overnight is a remarkable achievement of the sociological imagination.

4. For an expansion of this approach see Greer, *Social Organization, op. cit.*

5. Wendell Bell, "Social Choice, Life Style, and Suburban Residence," in W. A. Dobriner (ed.), *The Suburban Community*, New York: G. P. Putnam's Sons, 1958; see also Richard Dewey, "Peripheral Expansion in Milwaukee County," *American Journal of Sociology*, 53, 417-422. A similar argument is

made by Jaco and Belknap, in "Is a New Family Form Emerging in the Urban Fringe?," *op. cit.*

6. Greer, *Social Organization, op. cit.*

7. Sample survey data on the social role of the neighbor are reported in *Social and Political Participation in Winnetka,* by Scott Greer, James Holderman, Jr., and Peter McHugh (a Report of The Center For Metropolitan Studies at Northwestern University), Evanston: Center for Metropolitan Studies, 1961.

8. "The Social Structure and Political Process of Suburbia: An Empirical Test," Greer, *op. cit.* For a discussion of the interaction between population, association, and press, see Janowitz, *op. cit.*

9. Data supporting these generalizations are reported in Greer, "The Social Structure and Political Process of Suburbia: An Empirical Test," *op. cit.;* in Scott Greer and Peter Orleans, "Population Type, Social Structure, and Political Participation" (read at the Meetings of the Midwestern Sociological Society, Omaha, Neb., April, 1961); Greer, Holderman, and McHugh, *op. cit.;* and in Norton E. Long and Scott Greer, *Metropolitics: Illusion and Reality in Metropolitan Reform* (in preparation for 1962). The general theory is presented in more detail in "The Social Structure and Political Process of Suburbia," *American Sociological Review,* 24, 514-526.

10. In the Los Angeles areas studies by Greer and Kube, *op. cit.*, it was found that there was no variation in neighboring for working women, whatever the urbanism or familism of the neighborhood. It was low in all cases. But as the urbanism of the population increased (and therefore the proportion of working women in it) neighboring became progressively rarer among the nonworking women. They had fewer opportunities. Similarly, as the child population declined with urbanism, so did the proportion of children who played with other children in their own neighborhood. Here one sees clearly the effects of the residential area upon individual behavior.

11. Statistical evidence of independence at the macroscopic

level is presented in: Wendell Bell, "A Comparative Study of the Methodology of Urban Analysis," unpublished doctoral dissertation, University of California, Los Angeles, 1952; Maurice D. Van Arsdol, Santo F. Camilleri, and Calvin F. Schmid, "The Generality of Urban Social Area Indexes," *American Sociological Review*, 23, 277-284; Van Arsdol, Camilleri, and Schmid, "An Application of the Shevky Social Area Indexes to a Model of Urban Society," *Social Forces*, 37, 26-32; Maurice D. Van Arsdol, Ianto F. Camilleri, Calvin F. Schmid, and Earle H. McCannell, "Methods of Differentiating Urban Social and Demographic Areas," *Papers Presented at the Census Tract Conference*, Dec. 29, 1958, Washington: U.S. Department of Commerce, 1959, pp. 1-10; Walter C. Kaufman, "The Social Areas of Chicago," unpublished doctoral dissertation, Northwestern University, 1961.

12. For intensive studies of working-class informal association, see Floyd Dotson, "Patterns of Voluntary Association among Urban Working-Class Families," *American Sociological Review*, 16, 687-693; William Foote Whyte, *Street Corner Society*, Chicago: University of Chicago Press, 1943.

13. See Anderson, *op. cit.;* Paul G. Cressey, *The Taxi-Dance Hall*, Chicago: University of Chicago Press, 1932; Bell and Force, *op. cit.;* Bell and Boat, *op. cit.;* Bell, "Anomie, Social Isolation, and the Class Structure," *op. cit.*

14. Harvey W. Zorbaugh, *The Gold Coast and the Slum*, Chicago: University of Chicago Press, 1929. See particularly the description of the "dweller in rented rooms."

15. Similar results obtain with labor unions: the lower the social rank of the members the higher the probability of massification. See Greer, *Last Man In*, *op. cit.;* S. M. Lipset, M. Trow, and J. S. Coleman, *Union Democracy*, New York: The Free Press of Glencoe, 1956.

16. Shevky and Williams, *op. cit.*

17. Interaction of ethnicity and association is clear in such studies as Wirths' *The Ghetto*, *op. cit.;* Whyte's *Street Corner Society*, *op. cit.;* Elin Anderson, *We Americans*, Cambridge, Mass.: Harvard University Press, 1938; Walter Firey,

"Sentiment and Symbolism as Ecological Variables," *American Sociological Review*, 10, 140-148.

18. For a perceptive essay on ethnicity and national politics see Lubell, *op. cit.*

19. See Greer, "Catholic Voters and the Democratic Party," *op. cit.*

20. St. Claire Drake and Horace Cayton, in *Black Metropolis*, New York: Harcourt, Brace, 1945, emphasize the club life among Chicago Negroes. However, the narrow extent of voluntary organizational membership among urban Negroes (as disclosed in sample survey studies) leads one to conclude that such club life is at least as concentrated by social rank among Negroes as among other segments of the population.

21. The most urban and childless population studied by Greer and Kube, that of Central Hollywood, had come from the largest families of origin. (*Urban Worlds, op. cit.*) Something like a reaction against familism seem to have occurred among these people.

# *Chapter 5*

1. See the author's analysis of "The Citizen and His Local Governments: Central City and Suburban County," in J. C. Bollens (ed.), *Exploring the Metropolitan Community*, Berkeley and Los Angeles: University of California Press, 1961.

2. Greer and Orleans, *op. cit.*

3. Bollens (ed.), *op. cit.* "The Citizen and His Local Governments."

4. Greer and Kube, *op. cit.* For analysis of types of leaders named by a large suburban sample, see Greer, "The Social Structure and Political Process of Suburbia; an Empirical Test," *op. cit.*

5. For a spirited discussion of the self-selective process in Philadelphia politics, see James Reichley, *The Art of Government*, New York: The Fund for the Republic, 1959, pp. 94 ff. Sayre and Kaufman spell out, in detail, the nature of

the machine's control of the primaries and its dependence upon disinterest among the voters in Wallace S. Sayre and Herbert Kaufman, *Governing New York*, New York: The Russell Sage Foundation, 1960, as does James Q. Wilson, in *Negro Politics in Chicago*, New York: The Free Press of Glencoe, 1960. For a detailed study of the weakness and strengths of an old-time ward organization in an industrial satellite city, see Peter H. Rossi and Phillips Cutright, "The Impact of Party Organization in an Industrial Setting," in Morris Janowitz (ed.), *Community Political Systems*, New York: The Free Press of Glencoe, 1961.

8. For an older study, and a very influential one, see Robert S. and Helen M. Lynd, *Middletown in Transition*, New York: Harcourt, Brace, 1937, Ch. 3. For more recent studies, see those of Robert Agger and associates (particularly "Power Attribution in the Small Community," *Social Forces*, 34, 322–331) and Vidich and Bensman, *op. cit.* These are examples from a rather large collection of recent studies on small towns and cities.

7. Floyd Hunter, *Community Power Structure*, Chapel Hill, N.C.: University of North Carolina Press, 1953.

8. For an acute analysis pressing this proposition to its limits (and perhaps beyond them) see Raymond E. Wolfinger, "Reputation and Reality in the Study of Community Power," *American Sociological Review*, 25, 636-644. See also the review article by Herbert Kaufman and Victor Jones, "The Mystery of Power," *Public Administration Review*, 14, 205-212.

9. Kaufman and Sayre, *op. cit.;* Reichley, *op. cit.* E. Digby Baltzell, *Philadelphia Gentlemen*, New York: The Free Press of Glencoe, 1958; Long, "The Metropolitan Community as an Ecology of Games," *op. cit.;* Edward C. Banfield, *Political Influence*, New York: The Free Press of Glencoe, 1961; Martin Meyerson and Edward C. Banfield, *Politics, Planning, and the Public Interest*, New York: The Free Press of Glencoe; Wilson, *op. cit.;* Long and Greer, *op. cit.;* Linton C. Freeman, Warner Bloomberg, Jr., Stephen P. Koff, Morris

H. Sunshine, Thomas J. Fararo, *Local Community Leadership,* Syracuse, N.Y.: University College, 1960.

10. C. Wright Mills, *The Power Elite,* New York: Oxford University Press, 1956; Norton E. Long, "The Corporation and its Satellites," in Edward S. Mason (ed.), *The Corporation in Modern Society,* Cambridge, Mass.: Harvard University Press, 1959; Robert O. Schulze, "The Bifurcation of Power in a Satellite City," in Janowitz (ed.), *Community Political Systems, op. cit.*

11. Note the occupational position of the chief actors among the civic leaders in the six major Chicago issues analyzed by Banfield, *Political Influence, op. cit.* They tend to be either governmental bureaucrats, attachés to department stores, bank executives, office holders, ethnic leaders, or some combination of these roles.

12. Recorded by William L. Riordan, New York: McClure Phillips and Company, 1905.

13. V. O. Key, Jr., *Southern Politics,* New York: Alfred A. Knopf, Inc., 1949.

14. Long and Greer, *op. cit.* In truth, sample survey respondents mentioned Raymond Tucker, Mayor of the City of St. Louis, as an authority on the referendum issue more often, by several times, than all other political leaders combined. His image was authoritarian; reasons given for trusting him were his expertise, his character, his public spirit—with a strong hint that achievement of office was proof that he possessed these attributes.

15. Cf., Sayre and Kaufman, *op. cit.*

16. Janowitz (ed.), "Preface," to *Community Political Systems, op. cit.*

## Chapter 6

1. Most of these illustrations are drawn from Jerome Carcopinio, *Daily Life in Ancient Rome,* New Haven: Yale University Press, 1940.

2. Examples of metropolitan disorganization are drawn chiefly from my experience as Chief Sociologist with the Metropolitan St. Louis Survey, 1956–1957. Such experience was made more significant through the shrewd insight of Henry J. Schmandt, Assistant Research Director of the project. Some specific examples are given in my *Exploring the Metropolitan Community, op. cit.*

3. The phrase, "republic in miniature," is from Robert Wood, *Suburbia: Its People and Their Politics,* Boston: Houghton-Mifflin, 1959.

4. McKenzie, *op. cit.*

5. Government Affairs Foundation, *Metropolitan Surveys: A Digest,* Chicago: Public Administration Service, 1958.

6. Based on studies in St. Louis, Cleveland, and Miami, to be reported in Long and Greer, *op. cit.*

7. This discussion is based upon a study of Miami, as well as the generous help of Edward Soften, Ross Beiler, and Reinhold Wolff, of the University of Miami. They are not, of course, responsible for interpretation here.

8. For a revealing study of the interaction among the elite with respect to such a plan, see Matthew Holden, Jr., "Decision-Making on a Metropolitan Government Proposition: The Case of Cuyahoga County, Ohio, 1958–1959," unpublished doctoral dissertation, Northwestern University Department of Political Science, 1961.

9. These generalizations are based on a panel study of voters before and after the 1959 campaign for a Metropolitan District Plan in St. Louis and St. Louis County. Of three major and highly political provisions concerning (1) governance, (2) finance, and (3) jurisdiction of the District, only 10 per cent of a sample (selected for more than average political involvement) could give a roughly accurate resume of all three (cf. Long and Greer, *op. cit*). For further documentation of citizen incompetence (or indifference) in these matters see Amos H. Hawley and Basil G. Zimmer, "Resistance to Unification in a Metropolitan Community"; and Scott Greer,

"Dilemmas of Action Research on the Metropolitan Problem," both in *Community Political Systems, op. cit.*

10. When asked what kind of people voted for (or against) the District Plan, each faction said of the other side that they were "ignorant, corrupt, self-seeking, or politically irresponsible" (cf. Long and Greer, *op. cit.*).

11. Data supporting these statements are presented in the author's analysis of "Metropolitan Governmental Change: Support and Opposition," in Greer, *Exploring the Metropolitan Community, op. cit.*

12. Robert C. Wood makes a strong argument for these propositions in *1400 Governments: The Political Economy of the New York Metropolitan Region,* by Robert C. Wood, with Vladimir V. Almendinger, Cambridge, Mass.: Harvard University Press, 1961. See, also, *Suburbia, op. cit.*

13. Cf. Greer, *Exploring the Metropolitan Community, op. cit.*

14. Wood, *op. cit.,* has discussed these matters with perspicacity. See, particularly, Chapter 3, "Responses of Local Governments."

15. Wood, *ibid.*

## Chapter 7

1. Even plans and charters often do not have the consequences expected. See, for example, the way New York's "strong mayor" government tends towards a conservative federal system, according to one recent study (Sayre and Kaufman, *op. cit.,* especially in Chapters 17 and 18). As Norton Long has observed, there is no great reason to believe spatial integration would produce automatic functional integration—it would merely provide a change. It is a necessary but not sufficient condition for metropolitan polity.

2. According to Howard Brotz's theory of the relationship between politics and the class structure, it is *only* in the central city that the working class can expect a radical shift from

the ideology of Main Street. To be "first class citizens" whose interests are "legitimate" is a very great political achievement for the blue-collar worker and the Negro in the United States today; political fragmentation and political segregation may seem small prices to pay (Howard M. Brotz, "Social Stratification and the Political Order," *American Journal of Sociology*, 69, 571-578).

3. Banfield, *op. cit.*, documents the complex interaction of plenipotentiaries—politicians, bureaucrats, and civic leaders, against the background of the electorate, public opinion, and political folk-thought, for a number of major issues in Chicago.

4. Anthony Downs, "The Future Structure of American Cities," paper presented at the Conference on Transportation held by the National Academy of Sciences at Woods Hole, Mass., August 9, 1960 (reproduced).

5. Wood, *op. cit.*

6. Raymond Vernon, "The Economics and Finances of the Large Metropolis," *Daedalus*, Winter, 1961, pp. 31-47.

7. For a succinct discussion of the problem in terms of ecology (energy costs and location) see Cottrell, *op. cit.* Schmandt has recently argued the probability of progressive rigidification of suburban jurisdictional lines, corresponding to an increasing proportion of suburbanites who are employed outside the center and even in their own municipality (Henry J. Schmandt, "The City and the Rings," *American Behavioral Scientist*, November, 1960, pp. 17-19).

8. Raymond Vernon, *Metropolis, 1985*, Cambridge, Mass.: Harvard University Press, 1960.

9. C. Wright Mills, 1958.

10. H. D. F. Kitto, *The Greeks* (Penguin Edition, 1956), particularly Chapter 9, "The Decline of the Polis."

# INDEX